Ferdinand Burot, Maximilien Albert Henri André Legrand

The hygiene of the soldier in the tropics

Ferdinand Burot, Maximilien Albert Henri André Legrand

The hygiene of the soldier in the tropics

ISBN/EAN: 9783337134952

Printed in Europe, USA, Canada, Australia, Japan

Cover: Foto ©ninafisch / pixelio.de

More available books at **www.hansebooks.com**

INTERNATIONAL SERIES,

EDITED BY

LIEUT.-COL. ARTHUR L. WAGNER,

Assistant Adjutant-General, U. S. Army; late Instructor in Art of War at the
U. S. Infantry and Cavalry School, Fort Leavenworth, Kansas.

THE

Hygiene of the Soldier in the Tropics,

BY

F. BUROT,

Médecin principal de la Marine, Officier de la Légion d'honneur,
Officier d'Académie, Lauréat de l'Institut,

AND

M. A. LEGRAND,

Médecin de 1re classe de la Marine Chevalier de la Légion d'honneur,
Lauréat de l'Institut.

TRANSLATED BY

CAPTAIN GEORGE W. READ,

9th U. S. Cavalry.

No. 7.

TABLE OF CONTENTS.

	Page.
Introduction	7
Chapter I.—HABITATION	11
I.—Location of Troops in the Colonies	13
II.—Situation of Barracks and Posts	25
III.—Colonial Habitations	28
Chapter II.—ALIMENTATION	34
I.—Nutritive Value of the Ration	34
II.—Solid Aliments	38
III.—Liquid Aliments	43
IV.—Potable Water	45
Chapter III.—CLOTHING AND EQUIPMENT	58
I.—Rules of the Hygiene of Clothing	59
II.—The Different Articles of Clothing	61
III.—Maintenance of Clothing	66
Chapter IV.—MILITARY LIFE	68
I.—Occupations of the Soldier	68
II.—Fatigue Duties and Work	72
III.—Bathing	80
IV.—Amusements and Repose	81
Chapter V.—MEDICAL SERVICE	84
I.—Medical Personnel	84
II.—Hospitals and Infirmaries	90
III.—Matériel of the Health Service	92
IV.—Repatriation of the Sick	94
Chapter VI.—SANITARY POLICE	104
I.—Commission of Hygiene	104

	Page.
II.—Administrative Measures	106
III.—Hygienic Measures	112
Chapter VII.—SPECIAL MEASURES FOR EXPEDITIONS	120
I.—Colonial Expeditions	121
II.—Selection of Troops	124
III.—Convoys and Supplies	128
IV.—Sanitary Service	131
V.—Hygienic Conduct of Operations	164
Chapter VIII.—HYGIENIC PRINCIPLES OF A COLONIAL ARMY	174
I.—Recruitment	177
II.—Organization	188
III.—Departure for the Colonies	205
IV.—Length of Sojourn	206
Conclusions	209

PREFACE.

The importance of a knowledge of Military Hygiene on the part of officers in command of troops has long been recognized, and was painfully emphasized during the war with Spain by the heavy losses of many volunteer organizations that, remaining in home camps, did not see a hostile flag or hear a hostile shot. Not only is Military Hygiene a subject for serious consideration when our troops are stationed in a climate to which they are accustomed, but it becomes doubly so when they are called upon to serve in tropical regions whose climatic and hygienic conditions are new and strange, and where no enemy is so formidable as the endemic diseases.

The climatic conditions of Cuba, Porto Rico, and the Philippines are not unlike those of Madagascar, Tong-King, and Martinique; and the observations, experience, and deductions of the medical officers of the French Army in those regions are accordingly deserving of careful attention. It is reasonable to conclude that anything good or bad for a French soldier will be beneficial or injurious to an American soldier serving under like conditions, and the editor therefore ventures the hope that by placing this translation in the hands of his brother officers he may be, in some degree, conferring a benefit upon our military service.

Headquarters Department of Dakota,
St. Paul, Minn., June 13, 1899.

Hygiene of the Soldier in the Tropics

INTRODUCTION.

Much has been written of late years upon colonial hygiene. Numerous authors have tried to state precisely the rules to be followed in order to preserve the health of the soldier in hot countries. It would suffice to refer to their works, if we did not hope to present new ideas and to explain, in concise form, the *ensemble* of the measures capable of protecting the soldier against the diseases which Professor Brouardel has so happily called the *maladies évitables*.

The ideas which flow from our preceding studies permit us to face the danger and combat it rationally.

Among the means of protection and defense, the whole of which constitutes the Hygiene of the Soldier in the Tropics, it will not be surprising if we accord first place to those which seem to us more particularly shown to protect the European soldier from telluric action. The soil is the most important factor, for it is the receptacle of the germs which provoke the principal endemic disease: paludism. Water comes in second place; it bears the microbes of dysentery, of cholera, of typhoid fever; it is through it that epidemics are propagated.

There are other morbid causes which it is well not to neglect. The sun aggravates most of the diseases and produces some of them. The effect of high temperatures, of humidity, of cold, of insufficient or bad nourishment, of overwork, is only too real not to attract our most particular attention. The scarcity of medical attendance, the vicious organization of the sanitary service and of urban hygiene in the colonies, must also be taken into account.

The causes inherent to the country itself are not the only ones which produce mortality among the colonial troops; there are others peculiar to the individual who arrives for the first time in a tropical country, whether to remain in garrison or to take part in an expedition.

If the soldier is too young, if he has not a robust constitution, he will be an easy prey; but if, on the contrary, he has been selected strictly with a view to the trials he will have to bear, he will be able to become refractory to the morbid influences. There arises in this connection the much-debated question of the recruitment and organization of the colonial army. We propose to discuss it with all the care it merits.

Humanity and military interest are in accord in demanding, among the contingents destined for service in our possessions beyond the seas, a preparatory selection, which has not yet been made. There should no longer be allowed to go, even voluntarily, by the side of the veterans of the Sahara, of the Soudan, and of Chinese India, young Frenchmen entirely disarmed in the face of that enemy called the torrid climate. All should be professionals, inured to military life, capable of prompt and easy adaptation to the colonial existence, and surrounded, in addition, by all the guaranties necessary to the preservation of their health.

It seems to us possible to group in eight chapters all the hygienic principles applicable to the colonial troops, in the following order: 1st, Habitation; 2d, Alimentation; 3d, Clothing and Equipment; 4th, Military Life; 5th, Medical Service; 6th, Sanitary Police; 7th, Special Measures for Expeditions; 8th, Hygienic Principles of a Colonial Army.

It is a question of preparing a veritable *Code of Health*, and our ambition will be satisfied if we succeed in showing the absolute necessity, in the colonies, of a rigorous hygiene for both individuals and communities.

CHAPTER I.

Habitation.

It has been said by J. Rochard that an expense incurred in the name of hygiene is an economy. This is a truth which cannot be too well borne in mind when it is a question of providing the colonial soldier with a lodgment to protect him against telluric influences, inclemencies, and foreign contaminations.

To keep in good health in a warm country, it is necessary to be well housed and suitably installed. There are few of our colonies where it has been possible, from the beginning, to prepare a good installation for our troops, and there are none where hygienic reasons have exclusively determined the choice of the site.

At Martinique, Fort-de-France is built upon a marsh, while all around there are heights much better adapted for the establishment of Europeans. Saint-Pierre is built upon a contracted shore at the foot of the mountains; the pollution of the soil breeds dysentery.

In Guadeloupe, Pointe-à-Pitre is built upon marshy ground and at the bottom of a funnel; the unhealthfulness of this town is well known. Basse-Terre is better situated and has the advantage of having in its vicinity Camp Jacob, utilized so happily for the health of soldiers and officials.

French Guiana has presented, at certain times, a worse sanitary condition than that of Dutch and British Guianas, placed in the same conditions as to soil and climate; this difference can be attributed only to insufficient drainage and to the imperfection of the habitations reserved for Europeans.

In Senegal, the town of Saint-Louis, built upon an isle of sand, has long been deprived of potable water of good quality.

Gorée is only an islet, relatively healthy. Dakar can become a healthy town with an abundance of water. The post of Thiès, situated on the metaled road from Cayor, is hygienically placed at an altitude of 65 meters, far from all marsh, and is one of the best established.

Our establishments in the Soudan, Guinea, Côte-d'Ivoire, Bénin, and Kongo, leave much to be desired.

In Indo-China, great progress has been made. The town of Saigon, built over arroyos, has become habitable, thanks to a good system of canals of potable water, to large clearings, to the numerous plantations, to better-understood constructions, and to the wholesomeness of the soil. Tong-King will profit by the lessons of the past and will become a prosperous colony; if the heights are infested with paludism, while the Delta is destitute of malaria, the reason is that the Delta is admirably cultivated and the heights still uncultivated.

In New Caledonia, the town of Noumea, built upon a marsh, is exempt from paludism, but too often visited by typhoid fever and dysentery, which find in the geological formation causes favorable to their development. Tahiti is a volcanic island which would gain in salubrity if the habitations, more hygienically constructed, had been built a few hundred meters above the sea-level.

At Reunion, the paludism made its appearance about thirty years ago and shows itself with frequency in the towns of the littoral. And yet, upon the plateau of the mountain Saint-Denis, in a marvelous and easily accessible place, at an altitude of 400 meters, there is a site adapted for a superb town.

In our new possession, Madagascar, all points of the coast are unwholesome; this has long been known. The heights are habitable and capable of colonization, and, now that we are masters of them, we would be guilty not to utilize them.

In the colonies, more than elsewhere, when it is a question of habitation, the first care, when possible, is to select the site judiciously; in the second place, the best situation for barracks and posts should be studied; finally, it is important to regulate in all its details the installation of the buildings.

§ I. *Location of Troops in the Colonies.*

Our troops in the colonies usually live in the towns and our colonial towns are almost always located upon the littoral. There the troops are continually exposed to attacks of paludism, inevitable in the lowlands adjacent to the mouths of great rivers; to yellow fever, the endemic of the shores; to the possible importation, through commercial relations, of all the plagues coming from Europe, Asia, Africa, and America; typhus, cholera, etc.

In the great colonial centers, they are also exposed to the diseases of the civil population, European and native.

The English, those masters in the art of colonization, have, for a long time, understood the necessity of removing their soldiers from the littoral, and to this measure should be attributed, in great part, the diminution of mortality among them.

The Dutch have imitated them, and seem to have derived important advantages from this hygienic measure.

It is proper, in this point of view as in many others, to profit by experience and to utilize the examples set us by powers possessing, like ourselves, an extensive colonial domain.

ENGLISH STATIONS.

We cannot do better than to take a glance at the hygienic programme carried out in the colonies, by our neighbors across the Channel.

British India.—In Hindoostan, the English, for a number of years, have established *Health Cities*, which they also designate *Summer Stations*.

The point demonstrated is that the pure air of the heights has preserved the lives of thousands of soldiers.

Tables of mortality prepared for European soldiers prove how much easier acclimatization has become. Towards the middle of this century the European troops serving in India, although better cared for than during the wars of the past century, lost each year *one man in fifteen;* but since then the rate of mortality has constantly decreased.

India is one of the hottest colonies of the earth; the line of greatest mean heat—the equator—passes immediately to the south of the peninsula, and the isothermal line of 24 degrees bends around the northern plains, running along the first swellings of the Himalayas. The annual variation from one extremity of India to the other, more than 3,000 kilometers in length, is only 5 degrees centigrade, if the diversity of altitudes is disregarded and all stations are brought to the sea-level.

To obviate the serious inconvenience of these high temperatures during the summer and the depressing and febric action of the coast climate, the English have established, near the large towns of the littoral, secondary towns, which are used as summer residences. These are not, properly speaking, sanatoria for the cure of invalids, but are stations of preservation.

On the northern frontier, the Himalayan chain, a formidable barrier between India and Thibet, offers on its

Indian slope many favorable points for the establishment of health cities and important military posts. In southern India, the Western and Eastern Ghauts, gradually rising in terraces, from the narrow littoral to the ledge of a plateau 1,000 meters high, and joined together by the transversal chain of the Nilghiris or Blue Mountains, present equally, at a variety of altitudes, numerous sites capable of being utilized as summer resorts and sanitary stations. The question arises at the outset of connecting the selected points with the ports and principal centers by easy means of communication and of making it a study to eventually secure the development of these nascent towns.

PRINCIPAL STATIONS IN INDIA.

			Altitude.
Presidency of Bombay:		Poona	563 meters.
"	"	Matheran	749 "
"	"	Mahabalechwar or Malcompet	1347 "
"	of Bengal:	Darjeeling	2250 "
"	of Madras:	Bangalore	924 "
"	"	Outakamound	2200 "
Punjab:		Dharmsala	1950 "
"		Dalhousi	2243 "
"		Simla	2160 "
Koumaon:		Almora	1815 "
Indian slope of the Central Himalayas:		{ Ranikhet	1650 "
		{ Landour	2193 "
Ceylon:		Nouvera-Elia	1890 "

Poona, with an altitude of 563 meters, commands the region of the sources of the Bhima, and is one of the large cities of India; from June to November, when the monsoon blows and the rain falls in torrents, it becomes the temporary capital of the presidency of Bombay.

The station *Matheran* is situated, at an altitude of 749 meters, upon a butte completely separated from the chain of the Ghattes by the erosion valley traversed by the river Oulas; in less than four hours the inhabitants of Bombay can to-day reach the summit of the hill.

Mahabalechwar, one of the most frequented of the health cities of the Western Ghattes, is found in the district of Satara, at an altitude of 1347 meters. In spring it becomes the residence of most of the high officials of Bombay. During the warm season Mahabalechwar is very agreeable; it was founded in 1828, by a governor of Bombay, Malcom, and one of the villages of the station is named Malcompet.

From 10 to 15 kilometers from Madras, the two syenitic buttes called the *Monts Saint-Thomas* (where the governor's villa, noted for its gardens, is located) serve, like the plateaux of *Mysore*, as summer residences for Europeans. *Bangalore*, with an altitude of 924 meters, is considered one of the most healthful stations of the region; many English are established there.

South of Mysore, the town of *Outakamound*, the principal place of the Nilghiri, is of modern origin; its pleasure-houses are scattered over considerable space at a mean altitude of 2200 meters; to the east the escarpments of the Dodabetta, the Hotahiri, and the Kounour are likewise peopled by Europeans. Outakamound, following the example of the other English towns of India, has not less than three trial gardens for the culture of exotic species; these gardens are elevated at different heights upon the slopes of the plateau. The first cinchona plants were imported from Peru in 1860, and within a few years 25,000 of these plants were prospering in the environs of Outakamound. Now vast forests of quin-quinas have largely replaced the grasses and jungles of the plateau, and furnish the British Army an abundant supply of febrifuge.

Near Calcutta, *Hazaribagh*, a station renowned for its

fine air, is constantly gaining in importance as a summer resort for the English merchants of Calcutta who are kept in the neighborhood by business affairs.

Darjeeling is situated on the narrow edge of a mountain, and has an altitude of from 2060 to 2500 meters; 1800 meters below lies the gorge through which flow the waters of the Grand Randjit. This health city is 680 kilometers from the Anglo-Indian capital; the journey can be made in twenty-four hours by a railroad running from Calcutta to the foot of the mountain. The climate is very humid, the rains being almost daily. Like almost all the health cities of India, Darjeeling is flanked by barracks and batteries and constitutes an important strategical point. Elegant villas and luxurious residences have grouped themselves little by little around the barracks, and during the warm season become the homes of high functionaries, officers, and English merchants.

At an altitude of 2190 meters, upon a slope of the central Himalayas, *Landour* is also an important military station and noted town. It offers great advantages from the equableness of temperature, summer and winter, day and night; but during the rainy season it is exposed to all the violence of the monsoon and the rains are very frequent; in 1835, a German traveler, Hügel, saw it rain for eighty-five consecutive days.

Almora is situated on the Indian slope of the central Himalayas, in the basin of the Rampanga, an affluent of the Ganges, upon a spur of the mountains commanding a vast horizon. It is one of the towns preferred by the English on account of its elevation, 1650 meters, and the coolness of the air. Almora, the capital of Koumaon, has for its rival as a health city its neighbor, the modern *Ranikhet*, situated upon a plateau, at an altitude of 1815 meters, and offering (what nearly all other towns in the Himalayas lack) an abundance of water, level ground, and excellent materials for construction (stone and wood).

In the Punjab, upon a promontory of the last Himalayan chain, the British Government has founded a health city for its employees and soldiers. *Dalhousi*, at an altitude of 2243 meters, makes a superb observatory, whence the view extends over the beautiful valley of the Ravi, the mountains of Kangra, and the neighboring plains of Lahore and Amritsir. To the southeast, a buttress of the Dhaola-Dhar or "White Mountain" bears the pleasure-houses of *Dharmsala*, scattered between 1350 and 1950 meters along the mountain slopes. This other health city, which has replaced an antique Brahmin sanctuary, has become the chief place of the entire Kangra district and the center of numerous tea plantations.

Simla (35,000 inhabitants), situated at an altitude of 2160 meters, upon the Indian slope of the central Himalayas, occupies a separate domain between the provinces of the west and central Himalayas. Simla was founded recently, but the advantages of its position and the caprice of a viceroy of India have made it the summer capital for the whole empire. As soon as the hot season comes on, the routes leading from the plain towards Simla are covered with convoys and equipages carrying to the health city the high functionaries of Calcutta, followed by their employees; even some of the principal state officials emigrate every year at this time from the one to the other city. To the south of Simla, whose fame dates back scarcely thirty years, several other health cities have been built upon the slopes or crown the hills. These are *Soubathou*, *Kasnoli*, *Dagchai*, and *Kalka*, which are at the same time military stations.

The island of Ceylon, which likewise forms a part of the

great Anglo-Indian Empire, and is separated from the Deccan only by a narrow and shallow strait, merits mention from the point of view now occupying our attention. Unhealthy in the lowlands to the north of the island, in the plains, and along the shores which border the littoral, where the heat is insupportable in the hot season (the mean annual temperature being 27° to 28° Centigrade), the climate of Ceylon is very salubrious and most agreeable in the mountains of Pedrotallagalla and Samanala (Adam's Peak), whose summits attain 2200 to 2500 meters. The Portuguese, the former possessors of the island, and after them the English, have established their summer residences at points varying in altitude from 1000 to 1500 meters. In the hot season the Europeans and officials desert in a body the ports of Colombo, Pointe-de-Galle, and Trincomalee, repairing to *Kandy*, 518 meters in altitude, on a bend of the only river of the island, the Mahavila. When their business permits them to go farther away, they pass the hot season at *Nourera-Elia*, which has an altitude of 1890 meters.

It was very natural for the English to seek to establish these centers in the mountainous regions and upon the advanced promontories of the Himalayas, where it would be possible for them to recuperate their health, compromised by a sojourn in the burning plains of the Ganges and Indus, and to recover their strength, enfeebled by so debilitating a climate.

British Antilles.—In Jamaica, during the warm season, the English send their European troops to stations established at different points of the Blue Mountains, where the temperature is from 12 to 13 degrees lower than in the towns of the littoral, like Kingston, and where hygienic conditions are excellent.

The forests of Hope Gardens enjoy a great reputation

for healthfulness. There has been established at *Newcastle*, at an altitude of 1158 meters, a camp of preservation, to which is sent the greater part of the garrison during winter and in times of epidemic.

Western Africa.—A recent fact well shows the interest taken by the English in the solution of this problem of colonial hygiene.

They have resolved to establish a sanatorium for the West Coast of Africa, as a monument to the memory of Prince Henry of Battenberg; but they have not yet definitely decided upon its location. Some propose to establish it upon the continent itself, choosing an elevated locality between Cape Coast and Elmira; others wish to select an appropriate site on the Gran Canaria. At the present time, the last solution would seem to be much preferable to the first, for the Gran Canaria is much more accessible to the Europeans who live upon the West Coast of Africa than any locality in the interior. Moreover, it is reached by sea, avoiding all the dangers and difficulties of a journey across a pestilential country. Besides, the Gran Canaria, except in certain respects, is a very healthy place; it also offers all the alimentary resources of a civilized country, conditions which could not be found in the interior of Africa. A temporary stay in a sub-tropical climate like that of the Gran Canaria would be admirably suited to anaemic and paludal persons, and would perhaps be even preferable to an immediate return to the cold and humid regions of northern Europe.

When the Black Continent has been better explored, when routes and railroads have been established, it will not be impossible to have in the interior, far from the marshes of the coast, sanitary stations which can be reached in a few hours.

DUTCH STATIONS.

In their colonies in the Sunda Isles, the Dutch have likewise established sanitary stations.

At Java, to the south of Ambarawa, upon the first slopes of Merbaboe, at an altitude of 574 meters, is found the town of *Salatiga*, much frequented during the warm season; the climate is very agreeable and the view magnificent.

Tosari, at an altitude of 1780 meters, is the principal station of eastern Java; situated at an angle of an epaulment of the Tengger, it is much frequented by European officials and merchants on account of its climatic conditions.

Java possesses several other sanitary stations at altitudes varying from 1070 to 1800 meters, situated in well-chosen places, in the midst of a luxuriant vegetation; such are the sanatoria of Sindang-Laya, Buitenzorg, Tchiodas, and others.

The mortality of Europeans in Java is to-day ten times less than in the last century. Hygienic rules are more carefully observed; sites for habitations are chosen in healthy places, and the stations for summer residence, situated at various altitudes, permit a graduation of climate for valetudinarians and convalescents. Nevertheless one must know how to protect himself, by a strict *régime*, against certain diseases, particularly beri-beri, which now and then commits terrible ravages upon soldiers of every nationality composing the colonial army of Holland in the Insulinde.

FRENCH STATIONS.

In one of the French Antilles, Guadaloupe, the soldiers are not quartered habitually at Basse-Terre, nor at Pointe-à-Pitre, but at *Camp Jacob*. It is the only one of our possessions where it has been dared, up to the present, to openly break away from the customs of Old Europe. In fact, Guadaloupe has possessed, since 1841, Camp Jacob, situated at an altitude of 545 meters, above Basse-Terre and at the foot of the sulphur mine. The creation of this camp, due to the initiative of Admiral de Mosges, has been of considerable service, and has resulted, from a hygienic standpoint, in great progress. The mortality has become very light since the day it was decided to place the troops there.

At Martinique, the occupation of *Balata*, since 1869, has been only temporary and subordinated to circumstances. At Balata, however, as at Pitons, the benefits of altitude are lessened by the defective installation of the huts.

As for Senegal, the dissemination of the white troops takes place, for the garrisons of Dakar and Saint-Louis, only during the winter. The chief place of our possessions in Guinea, *Konakry*, seems to be happily chosen. The first buttresses of the Fouta-Djallon have been pointed out as relatively healthy. It appears that beyond Abomey there is a fertile country, favorable to European colonization and with an altitude of from 400 to 500 meters.

In Kongo, after having crossed the terraces traversed in cascades by the African rivers, Stanley and De Brazza found healthy plateaux where it would be possible for the European to live.

In Indo-China, at Reunion, and in Madagascar this question becomes of still more capital importance.

Indo-China.—It would have been possible at the beginning of the occupation to have avoided locating our troops in the lowlands of Cochin-China. To-day it is an accomplished fact, and making Saigon healthful has repaired the first error.

It would have been easy to have established stations upon the low heights of Cape Saint-James and also upon the hills of the islands Po-Condore, at an altitude of 350 meters.

In the heights the Europeans would find a cooler temperature, a purer atmosphere, and a more healthful soil.

This is true on condition that cultivation has caused the elements of paludism to disappear from the woods. Thus in Tong-King the high, wooded, uncultivated plateaux are more febrific than the Delta and cannot be utilized. It might be possible to make use of the lower altitudes of Dap-Cau, Quan-Yen, Bavi, and of the peninsula of Do-Son.

There is encountered between southern Tong-King and Annam, on the one hand the valley of Mekong and on the other a series of plateaux of variable altitude and extent which present exceptional conditions in point of climate, natural products, and general appearance of the country. These plateaux offer advantages pointed out for the first time by M. Harmand, and it is certainly there, in the future, after the indispensable work of clearing and grubbing has been done, that, after the example of the English, we will establish our Indo-Chinese summer resorts for our soldiers and European officials, in conditions of economy and with facilities which the stations of Simla and Outakamound do not present.

From this point of view, there may be specially cited the great plateau of *Boloven*, situated at an altitude of 950 to 1000 meters, between Bassac and the port of Tourane; that is to say, towards the very center of our possessions, and relatively easy of access. To put it in communication with the coast, a metaled road of from 200 to 250 kilometers would suffice, much shorter than the one which puts Calcutta in communication with Darjeeling. There can be found the most fertile soil, the conditions and climate of the south of Europe, pines, oaks, chestnuts, and elms; the extent of these mammillated plains is such that it would be possible to establish, in addition to residences and health cities, vast agricultural undertakings.

Reunion.—It would be easy to construct on the heights of Reunion stations for preserving the health of the soldiers who must pass several years in the island. Upon the mountains which stretch from the north to the south of Reunion, at a short distance from the coast, are already found places of convalescence well known to the inhabitants of Mauritius, who, decimated by fever in their own island, come there to regain their health. These are *Salazie, Saint-François, Cilaos,* and *Mafat.*

To-day there are military establishments at two of these easily accessible places of convalescence. Situated in one of the interior basins of the island, 52 kilometers from Saint-Denis and at an altitude of 900 meters, *Salazie* is a veritable sanatorium, where men already convalescent go to complete their cures. *Saint-François* is rather a summer station for the soldiers; situated on the flank of the mountain which overlooks Saint-Denis, and three hours from the latter town, with an altitude of about 400 meters, it possesses well-installed huts. This station, at a moderate altitude and in proximity to the chief place, would be found well adapted to accommodate the garrison permanently, like Camp Jacob in Guadaloupe.

Madagascar.—In our new possession nothing would be more useful than to establish sanitary stations for our troops.

Upon the coast there are no healthy points, with the possible exception of Nossi-Comba and Noss-Vé, on the west coast and Anjouan in the Camores.

On the east coast it may be said that all localities are unhealthy, not excepting Diego-Saurez.

But as a compensation, the mountainous buttresses approach the sea, and, without being obliged to mount to the summit of the plateau, we could create veritable "health cities," in the middle zone, upon the buttresses of the grand central chain, quite comparable to the Ghattes of India. This middle zone, inhabited more especially by Europeans, could be planted in coffee, cocoa-trees, etc.; tobacco, vanilla, corn, potatoes, and mountain rice could also be cultivated there. Our great colony, put in operation, would become a new India, and, like Java, would attain, in a few years, one of the first places as a coffee-producing center.

Interesting as are colonization and economic questions, we would wish, above all, that our soldiers, who assure the security of our colonial domain, be protected in the best possible manner against the endemic paludism, and we are convinced that this result would be obtained by utilizing the heights.

In speaking of sanatoria, we shall have occasion to show that the heights are far from being suited to all convalescents, still less to certain diseases; the coolness of the nights is relatively too sensible for those affected with anæmia, paludism, and, above all, with dysentery.

It would be wrong to demand of the climates of high altitudes curative virtues which they cannot possess; but their high degree of preserving power should be loudly proclaimed. It is in the heights, then, that the European troops forming part of the colonial regiments should be permanently stationed, save in cases where this is impossible. We will add that there would be profit in giving the native troops the same advantage of garrison.

§ II. *Situation of Barracks and Posts.*

The benefits of altitude are lost if care is not taken at

the outset to remedy the inherent defective conditions in geological formation or in the nature of the vegetation.

At Baria, in 1878, the establishment of a sanatorium on Nin-Din mountain was a complete failure; the hill not having been sufficiently prepared by axe and fire, the paludal or dysenteric patients taken there and quartered in the barracks, which were also defective, all felt an aggravation of their condition.

In Tong-King, on the road to Langson, the healthfulness of the posts differs essentially, according to the conditions under which they have been established. The precautions to be taken may be stated as follows: Avoid hills where heaps of organic matters in decomposition are found; choose in preference grassy plateaux; make the site healthy at the outset by clearing the trees, burning the brushwood, ramming the soil, and sodding. If these conditions are not fulfilled, the mountain, in spite of its lower temperature, will be inferior in healthfulness to a marshy but well-cultivated plain, such as is found in the Tong-King Delta.

It is not always possible to place troops upon high ground and it is often necessary to be resigned to quartering them in the plain. In this case special care should be taken in choosing the ground and in cleaning up the soil so as to diminish as much as possible its harmfulness to health. Humid ground, rich in organic matter, should be rejected. On the contrary, thick beds of sandy ground containing little soil should be sought. Land formed of hard limestone, of primitive rock, will be excellent if care is taken to level the basins in which mineral and organic *débris* accumulate and fermentation is produced. Both clayey and tillable ground should be discarded.

The soil should be drained if there are doubts as to its dryness. Artificial processes of drainage are familiar. A slight slope of the ground renders them easy and efficacious. Small trenches and collecting ditches, to drain the ground and carry the water to a river or to the sea, will suffice.

Wherever sanitation by cultivation may be attempted, the Algerian examples should be referred to and inspiration derived from the wise counsels of military hygienists.

Plantations which constitute a sort of natural drainage should not be in the immediate vicinity of the quarters, but at a certain distance, on account of the humidity. The eucalyptus and the bamboo seem to be most useful.

A judicious examination of the soil and subsoil, of pools of water with a tendency to stagnation, and of neighboring marshes, should be made. The fixed rule is: "The level of the subterranean water should be at least one meter below the surface."

It may also be said that the best orientation is east and west, with slight inclination to north and south, according to hemisphere and the prevailing breezes.

When troops have to be left in contact with an urban population, it is important to remove them as far as possible from the center of the towns and to place their barracks outside the inhabited zones. There, as everywhere else, they should be separated from rice plantations, marshes, muddy arroyos, slimy canals, and cemeteries. They should always be placed to windward of these causes of unhealthiness and sheltered from them by a screen of trees. The proximity of the sea-shore or of the banks of a river has its advantages and its disadvantages; there is an abundance of water and coolness; but, if the distance is not great enough, the humidity is to be feared, and also inundations.

Thus the situation of barracks or of a post is not a matter of indifference. Too often a question of pure convenience guides the choice of the persons called on to fix the sites of future military constructions. This is wrong. The work of the commissions is laid out, and if they bear in mind the principles we have just outlined, there will never again be built in the colonies a military establishment, no matter how modest, nor how temporary is to be its occupation, on the border of a marsh, in the dry bed of a river, or under the wind from an infected village.

In point of fact, the sacrifice of the most elementary hygienic precautions is hardly ever demanded by the necessities of war or circumstances beyond control, excuses behind which carelessness or incapacity find willing shelter.

§ III. *Colonial Habitations.*

With regard to colonial habitations, it is well to meditate upon the eloquent words recently spoken, at the Academy of Sciences, by M. Brouardel. Confined air is the great propagator of disease, in the same manner as the cohabitation of healthy organisms with those which are contaminated; the public powers and the corps of *savants* could not better employ their influence than by promoting more efficacious measures against unhealthy habitations. Recalling the Persian proverb, "Where there is neither air nor light, the doctor often enters," the eminent professor declares that infectious diseases are no longer caught in the hospitals, but in the town, and points out the means to be employed to diminish the number of epidemics.

In the colonies there is much more to be said and much more to be done. Hygienic mistakes are not lacking and great vigilance is required to protect Europeans from diseases arising from the bad appointments of the quarters. It will suffice to give some indication of the requirements of habitations appropriate for soldiers in the Tropics.

PERMANENT HABITATIONS.

Barracks should never be built hastily, as a simple shelter from the sun and a roof to keep off the rain; they should be, in every sense, a protecting, hygienic, and healthful lodging.

The colonial habitation should be built with the greatest care and of materials possessing sufficient resistance to withstand damage, as by the sun, rain, winds, meteors, humid or paludal soil, or the action of insects; if it suffers from these causes, the occupant would suffer more.

This is a principle too much ignored by builders who rely on the mildness of the climate and imagine that a simple screen interposed between the resident and the exterior suffices to protect him, without taking account of the danger from the proximity of a paludal soil.

Constructed upon dry ground, or ground dried by fire and carefully rammed, the barracks should be raised upon arches, or even upon piles, whenever it is too difficult to obtain perfect drainage. Cisterns, reservoirs, pumps—anything, in a word, which can hold moisture—should never be placed in barracks. Humidity, indeed, is the condition most favorable to the development of germs.

The walls should be very thick. The ideal building in a tropical country would be of granite or of cemented marble, and the conquering Spaniards divined the best means of having cool houses in their lavish use of hard stone and marble in their sumptuous palaces in Havana.

The walls should be painted, not white, but in light colors. It would be best to use oil paints, which vitrify the surfaces, facilitating cleaning and disinfection. The stairs should be iron, and wide passages should separate the apartments on each floor.

The flooring of the ground floor should be well raised, a meter at least, especially if there are no cellars.

The roofing should be double or doubled with a ceiling, and sufficiently inclined. In the colonies, shingles, thatch, zinc, and brick are used. The most commendable roofing is certainly one of fitted bricks, resting on imbricated and strongly fastened shingles. Terraced roofs would have more inconveniences than advantages.

A gallery is indispensable for each story. One sleeps inside the house, but one eats, receives, works—in fact, lives —on the gallery. The flooring of the ground floor should be continued under the gallery, and the materials, glazed or ceramic tiles, should be the same. It projects beyond the walls 3 to 4 meters and is supported by columns of brick, stone, or cast-iron. The interior wall should be that of the house itself, painted gray or light yellow; the external wall should be made of fixed or movable Venetian blinds, or even of matting blinds. It is well to have the gallery run all the way around the house; one of the sides will then always be shady.

All the windows should be *portes-fenêtres*, since all open upon the gallery. These large openings from floor to ceiling facilitate the renewal of the interior air. The outside shutters should have overlapping slats capable of being opened to admit the light; the interior doors should be glazed and ought to be closed at night. The rooms should be very large; the local accessories of the barracks should be on the ground floor.

Thus understood, the colonial barracks will secure to their occupants the best protection against the soil and against humidity, and will provide them, moreover, with space, air, and coolness. There will be sufficient ventilation if the roofs are provided with simple ventilators like those in the barracks of Hanoi, care being taken to provide for the case when they should be kept closed.

The electric light will be the future illumination of the large colonial barracks. The beds should have a simple metal lattice-work as a bottom; the mattresses should be of cocoa hair or granulated cork. Each man must have a mosquito net, a cupboard, and a bench or stool.

The annexes of the barracks also demand a great deal of care in their construction, especially the latrines. These should always be provided with movable *tinettes*, instead of fixed ditches, which infect the soil.

The preparation of store-rooms must not be forgotten, nor the kitchens: laundries, paved with flag-stones and provided with an abundance of water, with impermeable conduits to carry the dirty water outside the barracks.

The places of confinement for discipline should never be obscure and unhealthy.

Finally, a bath-house with a sufficient number of wash-stands on the galleries will complete the *ensemble* of hygienic barracks in the colonies.

TEMPORARY HABITATIONS.

Temporary use can be made of houses, temples, pagodas, factories, store-houses, barracks, and abandoned citadels. These are the *habitations of chance*.

In this case it must be remembered that aëration, cleaning, and, above all, disinfection are necessary to render them temporarily habitable, for they are usually very unclean and always open to suspicion. When necessary to construct temporary quarters, it is best to conform to the method of the country. *Paillottes*, huts of bamboo or of the leaves of the palm or ranevala, are of great service if the precaution is taken to erect them upon soil which has been cleared, rammed, and dried by fire. Care should be taken to make the buildings large, to have the walls and roofs thick enough, and to make the latter project all around the walls so as to form galleries. From time to time there is occasion to renew all except the framework, at least the straw and other vegetable materials of the roofs and walls, which become impregnated with humidity and exhalations, and form, for that reason, a receptacle for miasma. Finally, in case of epidemic, the commandant should not hesitate a single instant to abandon these quarters, which have cost so little, and consign them to the flames, while he erects others upon different ground.

Pisa and mud have some advantages, but only for temporary structures, to be used for a longer time than the simple *paillottes*, and which should therefore offer more resistance.

What is to be thought of ready-made huts, in sections, for the colonies? There is no lack of models: the pavilions of Moysart and Espitalier; the movable barracks of Ravenez; the tent of Docker, of Lefort, etc. In our opinion, solid and thick *paillottes* are better.

In Europe the hut may be of service; in our climate the heat is never torrid in summer; the rains have nothing in common with those drenching downpours, the common showers of tropical countries. In winter there is every facility for warming the interior of the quarters and for preserving a very supportable temperature. Is it the same in the hot countries? There the sun disjoints walls and roofs and warps metal plates; the water of the torrential rains infiltrates through the joints and crevices, the humidity corrodes the timbers and insects devour them. All these structures become heated to the point of being uninhabitable during the day, but become cool during the night. In a word, the model of the ideal hut for hot countries is yet to be found. While awaiting the realization of this hygienic desideratum, it would be possible to supply expeditionary columns with light and easily assembled metallic framework in sections. With straw, leaves, and branches, the screens could be rapidly prepared, and their juxtaposition would permit the erection of the huts with great facility of construction.

When it is absolutely impossible to raise the floor of the huts sufficiently or to have high camp beds, the ground, after being dried, should be spread with a thick litter of straw or dried herbs. The waterproof, which should always form part of the colonial equipment, could be used to envelop this improvised mattress. At any price, it is necessary to avoid not only contact with, but a too close proximity to, the paludal, humid, and contaminated ground, and the ideal, in temporary as well as in permanent quarters, is to remove the occupant from it as far as possible. It has always been known that, other things being equal, the upper floors of a dwelling are the most healthy. The same observation, apropos of paludism, has been made in the most fever-affected colonies, like Gabon, where those quartered on an upper floor have been completely protected from fever, while those on the ground floor were stricken without exception.

The very important statement may then be made, without fear of being taxed with exaggeration, that the most elevated dwelling realizes for individuals, in a malarial country, the excellent conditions obtained by communities, in the same country, by a constant residence in the hills—the hygienic benefit of altitudes.

CHAPTER II.

ALIMENTATION.

To preserve the soldier from telluric influences, to enable him to resist the attacks of paludism and thermic anaemia, the greatest care must be taken of his alimentation, and he must be assured the necessary quantity of the principal articles of diet. It is also averred that the bad quality of food, whether solid or liquid, is the principal source of disorders of the digestive organs. In other words, if it may be said that the prevention of paludism depends principally on habitation and accessorily on alimentation, the proposition may be reversed in the case of the second of the endemic affections of hot countries, and it may be said that if dysentery can be influenced in its origin and evolution by a defective abode, it remains, above all, an affection of alimentary origin.

§ 1. *Nutritive Value of the Ration.*

In hot countries, as everywhere else, the components of the ration should be combined in such a way as to secure the maintenance and reparation of strength. If properly composed, it should contain about 25 grams of nitrogen and 350 grams of carbon; that is to say, sufficient nitrogenous aliments, a suitable proportion of hydro-carbons, and enough fat to repair the tissues and maintain the phenomena of calorification.

At all times the soldier works enough to see his organic budget suffer greater losses by reason of perspiration and climatic fatigue than those suffered in Europe. Thus he must receive in hot latitudes a reparative alimentation, rich in hydro-carbons, abundant, and of good quality and variety.

There are also conditions demanding that the ration be greater in campaign than in time of peace.

Doctor Gayet fixes it thus for the two cases:
In peace..............23 gr. of nitrogen; 370 gr. of carbon.
In campaign...........26 gr. of nitrogen; 380 gr. of carbon.

In Tong-King in 1885, the ration of the European troops would have been insufficient if it had not been supplemented by good pay, which permitted the messes to buy poultry and vegetables. In fact, it contained scarcely 20 grams of nitrogen and 320 grams of carbon.

In Dahomey, these figures were somewhat greater, corresponding to 22 grams of nitrogen and 347 grams of carbon. The Europeans received 400 grams of fresh meat, in lieu of 300 grams, as in Tong-King.

In the Soudan, the ration of meat was 500 grams, which gave 24 grams of nitrogen and 342 grams of carbon.

A special ration has been issued to the garrison of Diego-Suarez since 1889. It is well composed, being equivalent to 26 grams of nitrogen and 380 grams of carbon; it is rich enough in nitrogenous aliments and contains a proper proportion of hydro-carburets, but includes only such fat as is indispensable. Doctor Reynaud considers it nearly the type to adopt for the hot countries. The composition of the ration in Madagascar, for the campaign of 1895, was based upon precedent, and established, it might be said, with great foresight; yet it contained only 100 grams of vegetables in place of 120, and 40 centiliters of wine in place of 60.

By decision of the Minister of War, dated January 11, 1895, it was fixed as follows:

RATION OF THE EUROPEANS.

Bread............................... 750 grams.
Salt................................ 20 "
Sugar............................... 35 "
Coffee, green....................... 24 "

Rice	40 grams.
Beans	30 "
Vegetable Soup	30 "
(Making 100 grams of Vegetables.)	
Meat	500 "
Tallow	30 "
Tea	4 "
Wine	40 centiliters.
Rum	4 "

The ration of wine was issued when possible; in the contrary case, a substitute was made of rum or of tea, or of sugar and coffee. It was estimated that this substitution would be necessary one day in two.

The Algerian tirailleurs could receive a ration of sugar in lieu of rum and wine; in this case they received no liquids.

Other substitutions were provided for urgent cases: ordinary bread could be replaced by 700 grams of biscuit or 600 grams of war bread; fresh meat, by 250 grams of preserved meats.

RATION OF THE MALAGASY TIRAILLEURS.

Bread	750 grams.
Fresh Meat	400 "
Beans	60 "
Salt	24 "
Rum	6 centiliters.

The 750 grams of bread could be replaced by 750 grams of rice, and the 60 grams of beans by 60 grams of rice.

The ration of the Houssa tirailleurs was identical with the above, excepting that the rum was replaced by 21 grams of sugar and 19 grams of green coffee.

The coolies received 800 grams of rice and 24 grams of salt.

The general commanding the expeditionary corps could order certain substitutions according to circumstances.

It is but just to acknowledge that the nutritive value of the ration was sufficient in Madagascar; if our soldiers had to suffer from lack of food, the fault was exclusively due to the difficulty of transportation.

The English, Dutch, and Italians have always had rations superior to ours: 28 grams of nitrogen and 308 grams of carbon, in the Soudan; 26 grams of nitrogen and 458 grams of carbon in Abyssinia.

We may state that the ration of 300 grams of meat is insufficient, not only in campaign, but also in time of peace. In the tropics "the soldier is always in campaign; if not against the enemy, at least against the climate." It is true that his food can often be improved by the mess or by the particular resources of the garrison; products of the poultry-yard, of the garden, of hunting and fishing; but these supplements are at the mercy of circumstances and can not be depended upon to relieve want in the companies. It is the duty of the State to foresee at all times the rational quantities to deliver to the men. In place of giving them the commodities, the money value might be turned over, when known that it is an advantage and a profit for them to draw all or a part of their rations from their own resources or from the resources of the country they inhabit. The eventual product of foreign resources should never be discounted in order to diminish the cost of the ration.

To sum up, we agree with Doctor Gayet, that the two types of ration to adopt, except as modified in detail by circumstances, should be as follows:

	In Peace.	In Campaign.
Fresh Bread............	750 grams.	750 grams.
Fresh Meat............	400 "	500 "
Dried Vegetables......	100 "	120 "
Wine..................	45 centiliters.	50 centiliters.
Rum...................	3 "	3 "

	In Peace.	In Campaign.
Sugar	50 grams.	50 grams.
Coffee	40 "	50 "
Salt	25 "	25 "

The peace ration contains 24 grams of nitrogen and 360 grams of carbon; that of war, 26 of nitrogen and 380 of carbon.

§ II. *Solid Food.*

It would be irrational to advise what has been called *indigenization* by diet; that is a condemned practice. Nevertheless, it is proper to remark that the most abstemious have the best resisting powers in the inter-tropical countries, and that the natives have a diet in which vegetables predominate.

The problem of alimentation in hot countries, says Navarre, is less to give the system its ration in nitrogen and carbon, than to give it in the most assimilable and least hurtful form. In fact, after a few months' sojourn in the Tropics, due to meteorological influences, the digestive functions become languid and the appetite diminishes. To give Europeans the ration which suits them, without producing a fatigue of the digestive organs, nitrogen will be demanded in preference to albuminoids of vegetable origin, and carbon will be borrowed from the hydro-carburets much more than from the fats.

A formula of admirable application to the dietetics with which we are now occupied is that of Trousseau. The most digestible food is the one which furnishes the greatest quantity of reparatory elements and requires the least possible work of the digestive forces. In recalling this formula we will say that the supplying of food of the one kind or the other is not a matter of indifference. Not only must the nutritive value of the food be considered, but also its more or less easy assimilation.

The quantity should be sufficient; the quality should likewise leave nothing to be desired. It is also important to give great latitude to receiving boards, and they should most attentively superintend the preservation of the commodities in the store-houses.

Bread, in order to be eatable and to furnish a healthful and savory food, should be made of well-dried flour, passed through the drying stove, and kept, not in barrels, but in perfectly soldered tin boxes furnished with braces of tough wood. If the flour turn sour in spite of these precautions, the damaged parts should be separated; then, after having subjected the parts known to be good to the heat of an oven at a temperature of 100 to 110 degrees, they should again be placed in the boxes which have been carefully cleaned.

The same recommendations apply to biscuit and war bread.

The mediocre quality of the meat, especially the beef, obtained in the colonies, due to the failure of pasturage, to insufficient care on the part of the natives, to the fatigue of the animal, often transported to its destination by sea or brought from a very distant region, demands careful attention on the part of the experts in order to eliminate animals with tuberculosis or scurvy, or those worn out or preyed upon by paludism. The slaughtering and bleeding of the animals must also be carefully supervised, as the flesh spoils much more quickly and easily than in Europe.

Dried vegetables, beans, lentils, and peas should not be punctured nor shriveled; their cooking ought to be prolonged and preceded by a soaking for at least twelve hours.

Sardines in oil and cheese are very nitrogenous and reparative foods, and are well suited, in certain cases, to contribute to the composition of a campaign ration. They are usually well preserved.

Preserved foods, also provided for the periods of operations, when the convoys and posts cannot be revictualed with the infinitely preferable fresh food, are principally preserves of beef, mutton, salted provisions, and vegetable soup. The preparations proposed, and those which are employed daily, are innumerable. Under the form of tablets, sausages of various kinds, and lozenges, they are able to render great service.

In their last campaign against the Ashantees, in 1896, the English used the *macomachie ration*, composed of mutton and vegetables seasoned with sauce, and the emergency ration, with a base of chocolate and solidified bouillon. Like fresh provisions, the preserved foods are subject to alterations. It is necessary to inspect the boxes, which warp in the store-houses, and to make sure of the solder, which ought to be pure tin, without traces of lead.

The salt foods, bacon and corned beef, have great disadvantages: they tire the stomach and excite the thirst. They ought to figure only occasionally in the ration, to vary the mess, or, in case of necessity, at the rate of two or three issues a week, as a complement to an insufficient ration of fresh meat.

Codfish is an excellent food and very nitrogeneous. It is open to the same objections as the salt meats, and should always be dry, odorless, and without trace of discoloration. The cooks should soak it in several waters before submitting it to a long cooking in boiling water.

There has lately been much discussion of the preservation of foods by cold, and of the service which this alimentary innovation, so useful in time of peace, might render in time of war. Upon the theatre of operations it is really much easier to transport an entire train of wagons loaded with food thus preserved, than a herd of animals on the hoof.

Besides the pecuniary advantage resulting from the small waste, the economy realized from the conducting *personnel* is considerable.

It would be curious to know if, at the time of an expedition to a hot country, this system of supplying the columns, by ships or by freight boats, could be utilized, and during how many days it would be possible to thus supply a column, which, unable to find cattle on the hoof in the place, should receive its provision of meat from the base of operations. There are, in this respect, curious experiments to attempt, the more easy because a number of colonies do not lack cattle, and because there are some among them, Madagascar for example, whose overproduction will render most useful service to the mother country in case of need.

In the authoritative opinion of M. Armand Gautier, the high temperatures of the tropical zones do not constitute an insurmountable obstacle to this method of supplying columns operating in the hot countries. Indeed, the commission of the 30th of May, 1890, appointed by the Minister of War to study the preservation of meats by refrigeration, concluded that meats frozen at 10 to 15 degrees and then kept in store-houses cooled to below zero (Centigrade) could be preserved indefinitely, transported as a loose cargo in ordinary wagons, even in summer, and consumed several days after thawing—could, in a word, furnish, in time of peace as in time of war, an excellent supply, having all the qualities of fresh, muscular flesh.

Meats preserved by cold have a composition analogous to that of the best meats and undergo no sensible change. The taste is little modified and attention is required to distinguish these meats from the fresh; they are even more nutritive, quite as digestible, and, what is an important fact contrary to popular belief, they do not putrefy at once after thawing.

The process of preserving by refrigeration can be applied to game and poultry, and especially to eggs, milk, fruits, and vegetables. In England, milk arrives from Canada, frozen in enormous blocks. Cannot the alimentation of troops in campaign in the colonies find in the utilization of these methods of preservation, perfectly applicable to the store-houses of our colonial cities, precious resources for future expeditions?

A word upon *dynamogenic* or *accelerative* foods, which have to a high degree the property of exciting the muscular and nervous systems. They are calculated to keep in breath, for long hours, men given up to intense work.

Heckel has manufactured condensed accelerative rations, containing all the elements for the alimentation of a fighting man and sufficing to give him a strength capable of long marches. These rations are composed of meat powder and Kola nuts. They are in the form of a bar of chocolate or of biscuits, and weigh 25 grams. Their price is 3 fr. 25 per kilogram. From trials made up to the present, it appears that these rations can be utilized at a given moment; but it is better to employ them only as companions to the ordinary rations, on account of the dislike and digestive troubles which result from their habitual use.

We have recommended the most attentive supervision concerning the quality of the components of the ration. These precautions are not less necessary with regard to all commodities, whether animal or vegetable, coming from purely local sources. At military posts, as on board ship, the doctor, or, in default of one, an officer, ought to use the utmost care in regard to the food—game, vegetables, fruit, and fish consumed by the tables.

In the colonies, there are poisonous fruits which should be known. Nor should it be forgotten that in hot countries, several species of fish are to be rejected as capable of causing trouble, especially at certain seasons.

A condition concerning living which may appear accessory, yet is important in a hot country, is the variety and proper preparation of food. It is not what one eats, but what one digests and assimilates that nourishes and repairs. In countries where loss of appetite is experienced the best stimulant to oppose to the inertia of the stomach will always be the skill of a good cook. Now, without going into too much refinement, a post commander should superintend the cuisine of the men and direct the inexperienced European cooks and, with even more reason, the native Vatels. He should satisfy himself, personally, in regard to the manner in which the food is prepared, and as to its cleanliness, cooking, and seasoning. He should remember the precautions to be taken with regard to salads, cucumbers, radishes, and other products usually consumed in a raw state. Orders should be given and strictly carried out that they should never appear upon the tables without having been thoroughly washed and stripped of the least traces of impurities which might conceal the germs of dysentery and typhoid. Even more than in France, it is desirable that the soldiers should have utensils in good condition and scrupulously clean.

Finally, the meals should be regular and taken at the same hours in proportioned quantities. Regular habits should not be unnecessarily changed. An excess of food may be attended by serious consequences, resulting in gastric embarrassments and slight fevers.

§ III. *Liquid Aliments.*

Wine, brandy, tea, and coffee constitute, with water, the only beverages useful in the alimentation of troops.

Wine is an excellent and hygienic drink, and we have seen that it forms part of the ration of the colonial soldier.

The troops in France do not receive wine in time of peace; the heavy war ration provides for the daily issue of 25 centiliters.

In the colonies wine is issued daily; the ration is 40 centiliters in ordinary times, but has often been increased to 50 and 60 centiliters in campaign.

Wine, containing alcohol, tannin, glycerine, sugar, vegetable acids, and salts of iron, soda, and lime, is at once excitant and tonic. It quenches thirst very well, especially when mixed with water, and sustains and revives the strength on occasion. For all these reasons we are of the opinion that it has its marked place in the ration of the colonial soldier.

The wine should be of excellent quality with no alcohol added. It should not be "doctored" nor adulterated in any way with poisonous substances, such as litharge, salicylic acid, fuscine, etc. It ought to contain from 12 to 13 per cent of alcohol, as that quantity is indispensable to preserve it in a hot country. Unfortunately, these conditions are very difficult to exact rigidly from the dealers, on account of the purchase price. The wine may be very acceptable, at least to the taste, when it is received by the colonial boards; but it deteriorates rapidly under the heat; it sours in the casks. It has been suggested to have it delivered in bottles packed in boxes; the trial has succeeded in the Soudan; but it can be a question of small quantities only, to supply the weak effectives. Pasteurization by cold, by the Chamberland filter system, might be of service if it were more practical and less burdensome.

When the resources permit, on days of march or fatigue, there is no harm in doubling the wine ration at one of the meals, as is the custom aboard ship.

Partisans of wine, we are not at all so of rum or brandy,

whether ashore or at sea. This is a beverage to be reserved for the sick and for those suffering from cold or wet. Even then it should only be given mixed with an infusion of tea or coffee. Of these last, on the contrary, the quantities issued should be very large, for there can be no bounty more profitable to the man than the greatest possible allowance of tea, coffee, and sugar. When the wine gives out, it is still with this form of alcoholized infusions, and not with pure alcohol, that the ordinary beverage should be replaced.

To do otherwise is to seem to point out to the soldiers the necessity of pure brandy in the alimentation of the hardworking man, which is both contrary to hygiene and an encouragement to alcoholism.

In our time, the tendency to consume alcohol of all qualities and at every opportunity is, unfortunately, only too extended, and the best means of preventing its abuse later would be to prove to the men that the use of pure alcohol is in no sense necessary to the health and that it may be dangerous. An evident fact, and one which we have brought to light in the statement of the causes of the diseases of the soldiers in hot countries, is the indisputable influence of alcoholic habits, chiefly the use of rum, in the production of haematuric bilious fever, hepatitis, and sun-stroke, and in the aggravation of entero-colitis.

§ IV. *Potable Water.*

It is a current custom among the soldiers to charge to the account of the drinking-waters consumed in this or that colony almost all the affections contracted beyond the seas. The natives in many places agree with them in this. In Upper Tong-King, the Annamites formally accuse certain waters of causing a swelling of the spleen when drunk in the crude state.

Now, with the exception of fevers and paludism, the

germs of which, from all evidence, are taken up in the air by the respiratory organs, it is certain that the popular belief is well founded.

A commander who can provide his men with an absolutely potable water may be almost sure, in all circumstances, of preserving them from dysentery, hepatitis, typhoid fever, and cholera, and of protecting them against the less grave affections of which the eggs of tænia and ascaris, the germs of filaria, the fillets of blood-suckers, etc., are the most frequent causes.

When one has seen the ravages occasioned by diseases of hydric origin, he is convinced that in peace, as in war, and even more in the colonies than in France, the question of water is *capital*. To the same degree as the active prophylaxis of malaria, it forms a stratum of the foundation upon which good and true military hygiene must rest.

Always, in all circumstances, a commandant should ascertain if the water is potable and have means at his disposal to render it pure or to improve it.

CHARACTERISTICS OF POTABLE WATER.

A potable water is a water which is pure from both a physico-chemical and bacteriological point of view. These two conditions are absolutely indispensable.

Physically and chemically, a pure water is fresh, clear, odorless, and tasteless. Vegetables cook well in it and soap lathers.

By this standard, the type of potable water is that from a running spring; then comes rain-water caught directly at the time of its fall in a drinking-glass; the water of clear rivers, collected from the middle of the stream far from the accumulations which may gather upon its banks, or at least above such agglomerations. The water of deep wells, covered and removed from habitations, is also, when they are well kept, a chemically potable water. Finally, distilled water, when it has been aërated, likewise represents an excellent type of potable water, utilized aboard ships.

The senses and culinary and domestic use enable one to speedily discover if the water from these various sources possesses the necessary qualities to give it the physico-chemical value of a potable water. Reciprocally, it is easy to reject at the outset those which do not fulfill these conditions; such are the waters of marshes, ponds, torrents, rivers which are muddy and foul, the water of certain springs and of certain wells, which does not cook vegetables and makes no lather with soap, because it is silenitic—that is to say, charged with sulphate of lime.

It is not sufficient for a water to be pure from the physico-chemical standpoint to make it potable; it must also be pure from the bacteriological standpoint—that is to say, it must contain no foreign organic matter, especially any pathogenic organism. Now, the waters which are purest in appearance may have been defiled or contaminated, whatever their source, during their passage or their stay upon roofs, in conduits, in reservoirs, closed or open. This pollution of water chemically pure may result from infiltrations from the neighboring soil or from germs diffused in the atmosphere, whether under usual conditions or in time of epidemics. A bacteriological examination alone can detect the presence of these pathogenic micro-organisms; but without having recourse to a microscopic analysis, the impurity of any water whatever can be discovered and the presence of suspected organic matters revealed if they are sufficiently dangerous to necessitate the rejection of the water. This result is obtained by one of the following methods:

1. A very concentrated solution of tannin (reagent of Hager) is prepared; 20 grams of this solution is added to a

large glass of water and allowed to stand. If the water becomes turbid in less than an hour, it must be rejected.

2. Pour into a glass of water two or three drops of a 1:1000 solution of permanganate of potash. If the solution becomes discolored—that is to say, loses its beautiful roseate tint, the water is not potable.

A further examination is necessary, if it is desired to be entirely informed and to seek the nature of the organic elements, suspected or otherwise, contained in the water, or the presence of this or that microbe.

It is therefore easy to ascertain the quality of any water under any circumstances in which one may be placed, and to know, in a word, whether or not a water is potable.

MEANS OF PURIFICATION.

It sometimes happens, especially in the colonies, and principally in campaign, that the commanding officer will have neither the time nor the means to have the water analyzed; he will then have doubts about its quality, from ignorance of its source or from other unknown conditions as to its origin. Sometimes, the circumstances in which he is placed, as in an epidemic or in defective sanitary conditions, impose increased precautions. Finally, it may be that the troops have at their disposal only a water which is manifestly not potable, as the water of a pond or of an unclean or badly situated cistern.

In all these cases the absolute purification of the liquid given to the troops, for all alimentary uses, becomes a necessity of the first order. How can this important problem be practically solved?

There are a great many ways of purifying water; we will point them out briefly.

Steeping in alum has been employed in the extreme Orient from time immemorial. It is of service in countries where the waters are very earthy; but, in order that this process may be effective, it is necessary that the *dépôt* where the alum is made should have time to produce it. Now, as M. Laveran observes, the soldier needs a rapid process for purifying water. Steeping in alum destroys or precipitates only a part of the germs in suspension.

The other processes heretofore employed have given only incomplete results. These processes, but little used in campaign, are: *sterilization* by heat; *distillation*, which requires special preparations, cumbersome and costly; *boiling*, which the army doctors have recommended for the past hundred years, while admitting the inconvenience and difficulty of execution.

The same objections apply to *filtration* with filters of all kinds, however improved they may be, heretofore utilized. They are costly, fragile, and unmanageable.

Charcoal and amianthus filters (Maignen, Brayer) clarify the water, but permit the passage of pathogenic germs.

The Chamberland filter, called *the Campaign*, is heavy, difficult to transport with the column in a hot country, and subject to deteriorations which rapidly render it unserviceable.

Trials made during the Dahomey and Madagascar expeditions show that this filter is useful only in garrison.

Besides, neither the Chamberland nor Berkefeld filter can be used by isolated men. The traveling filter (Chamberland system), which can be taken apart and is contained in a tin box, and is composed of one or more *bougies* joined in a collector, is too delicate and complicated for the soldier. At most it might be suitable for officers and explorers supplied with spare *bougies*.

In Dahomey, several filters of various models were placed at the disposal of the senior commanding officer;

among them were the Chamberland and Maignen, a system consisting of a sort of funnel furnished with a felt diaphragm. It was very quickly seen that the Chamberland filters, while useful in a hospital, a stationary ambulance, or a detached post, were impractical for troops in campaign; the *bougies* became foul and the best of cleaning did not restore the filters to their primitive condition. The officers gave the preference to the individual filters, the canteen filters, or the squad filters of charcoal and amianthus. There are several practical points in favor of the Maignen filter. If there should chance to be a deterioration of the apparatus, warning is immediately given by the black color of the liquid and the damage can be repaired. It is also easy to manufacture all the parts of a similar apparatus, if there is a reserve of amianthus and charcoal.

At the time of the Madagascar campaign, it was not known what filter to recommend, and none was adopted. The ministerial instructions prescribed the clarification of turbid water by the use of alum, by straining it through a cloth, and by boiling. The daily ration of tea was designed to insure the latter effect. For boiling the water special pots were provided; it was never to be boiled in the pots used for making soup, as the water then contracts a taste of burnt meat, which prevents the men from drinking it.

These measures, the use of alum, straining, and boiling, were often neglected, because it takes a great deal of time to make boiled water cool.

Distillatory apparatus impose a great expense for purchase and setting up; their management requires experienced men, and their maintenance is costly. They can be employed only at the base of operations, and should be installed at the beginning of the campaign, before the arrival of the troops.

Admiral Bienaimé made an excellent use of a distillatory apparatus which had existed for a long time at Tamatave; he caused it to be set up at Majunga, in 1895, and the soldiers of the expeditionary corps benefited by it.

PERMANGANATE REDUCING-FILTER.

Impressed for a long time with the inconveniences inherent in the different methods proposed and used in turn for the purification of drinking-water for troops in campaign in the colonies, our colleague, M. Lapeyrère, principal pharmacist, has undertaken a series of laboratory studies which have led to a most happy result.

Taking for his calculations the essays of Burlureaux, Girard, Bordas, Babès, Langlois, Girardin, etc., upon the use of powders with a base of permanganate, he succeeded in deducing from their combinations a process which we must particularly describe.

Principle.—This process may be considered as the synthesis of two methods of purification—sterilization and filtration.

The rapid and complete sterilization of water with a special powder, described below, has been demonstrated by experiments made at Rochefort, in the bacteriological laboratory, and at Paris, by MM. Laveran and Hanriot, of the Academy of Medicine.

This powder is thus composed:

Quicklime*..	0 gr. 05
Crystallized alum, dry...............................	0 " 12
Soda carbonate, dry..................................	0 " 10
Permanganate of potash...........................	0 " 03
Total..	0 gr. 30

*Chaux vive délitée.

These 30 centigrams represent the average dose to the liter, which may be given by a little measure of the same capacity.

Alum enters into the composition of the sterilizing powder, as it is necessary to clarify the water of rivers. This acid salt forcibly combines with the carbonate of soda and a small quantity of lime, alkaline substances, which, in the presence of water, enter into chemical action with the double sulphate of alumina and of potash.

The filtration, the object of which is to remove with the earthy excess in suspension in the water the excess of reagent, is accomplished by means of a reducing-filter of the greatest simplicity, based upon the property possessed by woolen texture impregnated with oxide of manganese, to reduce the permanganate of the reagent in excess in the water to be purified.

Mode of Operation.—By the aid of a little measure, the sterilizing powder is thrown into a carafe of water about five-sixths full.

The liquid, which has become rose-violet, is shaken, and if at the end of five minutes the color persists, it only remains to filter the water by aid of the reducing-filter.

If the rose color of the liquid disappears, a second measure of the sterilizing powder is added; and this process is continued until the rose persists.

When this persistence of the rose is obtained, it is an assurance that the water is sterilized.

Then it is filtered. The filtering medium is very simply composed of flannel with a long nap, impregnated with sesquioxide of manganese, and then rolled up like a cigar and encased in a box of small dimensions. This metallic box is of aluminum, from 6 to 7 centimeters long by 18 millimeters in diameter. It is open at one end and closed at the other by a metal ring, through which runs a short pipe, to which is fitted a rubber tube to act as a siphon. In the colonies the rubber tube would be replaced by one of impermeable fabric.

The woolen flannel of the Pyrenees gives good results. It is made reductive by alternate saturations and cleansings of permanganate of potash.

The thickness of the filtering mass is represented in this filter by the length of the box used, and the reducing power by the degree of purity of the wool and the proportion of oxide which it retains. As to the rapidity of the filtration, it naturally depends upon the degree of permeability of the texture and also upon the length of the rubber tube. For the individual filter, the rapidity is sufficient to obtain a liter in fifteen minutes on an average. In order to filter the water which has been sterilized, as indicated by the persistence of the rose color after the addition of the sterilizing powder, the filter is plunged in it and the siphon primed by aspiration. It only remains to collect the water in a glass, a measure, or a carafe. The water which flows from the tube, clear and limpid, is absolutely potable.

To clean the filter there is the same simplicity of process. It is sufficient to withdraw the flannel from the box and to wash it, rubbing it between the hands, after having dipped it into pure water or water to which the sterilizing powder has been added. It is then rolled up again like a cigar and replaced in its receptacle.

Scientific Value.—This system has been submitted to the "Conseil supérieur de santé de la Marine," which has accepted it in principle. The Academy of Medicine also took up the question and appointed a commission, which made a favorable report.

MM. Laveran and Hanriot are satisfied that the pathogenic microbes which most often contaminate water (bacillus of typhoid and spirillum of cholera) are destroyed in water purified by this process. Certain sporular microbes resist, but they are always non-pathogenic.

On the whole, sterilization by this simple and really practical process is sufficient.

Some criticisms of detail have been made regarding the composition of the powder, which, however, has been modified.

It might be feared that the powder would be altered by the air, or would obstruct the pores of the filter by the precipitates, and thus rapidly diminish the delivery. Nothing is easier than to protect the powder from the air by a well-closed box.

The fouling of the woolen flannel is not to be feared. It is easily cleaned and its daily washing ought to be an obligation. Has it not been said, with reason, that the best filters are those which became fouled most easily, because this is the proof that they play their part perfectly, and therefore impose the duty of cleaning them often?

The action of the sterilizing powder upon metals is not to be feared. It does not attack inoxidizable metals, and the deposit of oxide of manganese which may form upon these metals is absolutely inoffensive and can be easily removed by washing.

With M. Laveran, it may be said that the Lapeyrère system marks a real progress in the important question of the purification of water.

Application to Troops in Campaign.—The individual or pocket filter, such as has just been described, possesses the following desirable qualities: absolute decoloration of the permanganate of potash, rapidity of filtration, limpidity of the filtered liquid, lightness, solidity, and ease of manipulation and cleansing.

It was a question of making it practical for the soldier in campaign, and M. Lapeyrère thinks he has succeeded.

The soldier's filter differs from the pocket filter only in its greater length. It can be put into the canteen of the regulation model, whence its name—"*bidon-filtre*."

It is fixed either permanently or temporarily to the cork of the large opening of the canteen by a metal aspirator tube. This tube passes through the cork and extends several centimeters outside.

The canteen also has an inoxidizable metal flagon fixed on one of its faces, with a capacity of about 35 cubic centimeters, containing the permanganate powder; a little measure is hooked on the interior of the hermetically sealed cover of the flagon.

In case of a beverage which requires neither sterilization nor filtration, the filter remains closed and the soldier drinks from the ordinary opening of the canteen.

If it is necessary to filter the water, the soldier fills his canteen, pours in a measure of the permanganate powder, puts the filter in place and shakes the canteen violently. He can drink directly from the canteen, or, after putting on the aspirating tube and placing the canteen upon an elevated place, his knapsack for example, he can start the flow of water by aspiration and receive the sterilized and filtered water in his quart cup.

After the canteen has been used about ten times, the filtering medium should be withdrawn and cleaned. This can be done while resting during the halts; the canteen itself should be purged of all deposit and washed with water containing one or two measures of powder, to destroy the organic matter which might adhere to the walls.

M. Lapeyrère has busied himself with remedying certain material imperfections pointed out in the report of the

Academic Commission. It will be possible, for example, to find a way to protect the powder from the rain and to prevent the box from forming a troublesome projection. It is easy to keep the apparatus in repair; it must be acknowledged, however, that the purification of the water intended for drinking will be best assured if it is made for a group of men, as a squad or a company. If it is left to individual initiative, without supervision, it will yield the least desirable results; it is the same with the most elementary hygienic prescriptions. As surely as the methodical use of an efficacious process is prescribed by authority, cases will be seen where, escaping all supervision, the soldier will consume non-purified water.

The great merit of the reducing-filter is its extreme simplicity. It is at everybody's door; it can be purchased or constructed at little expense; it can be operated and cleaned with the greatest ease.

The necessary materials to make one can be found everywhere and always. There is not a colony whose market cannot furnish the sterilizing powder and prepared woolen flannel, or at least fine and well-cleaned sponges.

The most simple filters have always been the best. The troops in Abyssinia were recommended to take a small linen cloth, make a sack of it, fill it with powdered charcoal, join to it a tube plunged to the middle of the filtering substance, dip the sack in the water to be filtered, and suck the water through the tube.

The system we have just studied is more scientific, but quite as simple. We believe it is destined to render great service to the colonial troops, in the garrison towns, and, above all, during expeditions.

Up to the present, filtration alone has not been able to act upon the soluble morbid organic agents, such as the toxines and the alkaloids. The permanganate of potash connected with filtration has a very great advantage in improving water for drinking.

Alimentary hygiene is easier to observe than the hygiene of habitation. Individual initiative is here all powerful, and it can not be too much developed by teaching each one what he ought to do to avoid the diseases whose germs are absorbed by the digestive organs.

CHAPTER III.

Clothing and Equipment.

"Not to get cold is to avoid almost certainly all the causes of disease." These words of General Wolseley ought to be inscribed in the rooms of our colonial barracks in the same manner as the English inscribe upon their wharves in India: "Beware of the Sun."

Indeed, if certain parts of the apparel, like the helmet, are intended to prevent sunstroke; if the shoes ought to assure the protection of the feet and the lower limbs against insects and the asperities of the soil, the principal *rôle* of the clothing is to prevent the loss of the heat accumulated by the body within. It is precisely because one is warm and is often in a perspiration in the colonies that one needs to be covered; without overloading the body with too heavy and thick materials, it is necessary to cover it to avoid the currents of air. A too rapid evaporation of the perspiration from the surface of the body chills it; there is the danger. A man who is cold is on the verge of disease; he is more susceptible to simple diarrhœa, to dysentery, to hepatitis, to an access of fever, and to physical disorders generally. They declare themselves in him as soon as a sufficient cause shows itself; if they already exist in a latent state, their evolution is immediately accentuated.

The clothing of the soldier in the colonies has been the object of wise modifications; it might be improved still more and be more specialized in certain circumstances. Notwithstanding the improvements made, the last word has not been said.

§ 1. Rules of the Hygiene of Clothing.

The principal rules of the hygiene of clothing for the colonies may be stated as follows:

Wear warmer clothing in the evening and at night than in the day; always wear a flannel band at night; wear a helmet or equivalent head-covering from morning to evening; have extra shoes to wear after the march; use an equipment which neither overloads nor compresses any part of the body.

It is not long since soldiers in the far East were clothed almost the same as in Europe. Before 1860, the colonial troops were furnished with no light clothing except white trousers.

During the campaigns in China and in Mexico, the troops made use of a cap covered with white linen and with a havelock of the same material.

Later, in Cochin-China, they adopted the straw hat and the native *salako*. Shortly afterwards a trial was made, for the garrisons of Senegal and Cochin-China only, of a paletot of special flannel, for ordinary wear.

In 1873, the large flannel belt was given to all the soldiers in the colonies.

It was not until 1878 that really important measures were adopted. The different head-coverings were replaced by the cork helmet covered with white linen; the cap was kept only for morning and evening wear, night guard-duty, and traveling. The flannel jacket was made regulation for all our possessions. Flannel trousers were tried and subsequently adopted. The large red belt was replaced by a small white one worn directly over the flannel vest.

In 1883, the flannel dolman was adopted for the use of officers and adjutants. It was the day dress for drills and campaign, the dolman of France being always reserved for full dress.

By a decision, in 1886, every man in the colonies received for wear during the daytime a paletot of linen or cotton twill of a brown color. With the helmet, the trousers, the gaiters of cloth, and the flannel belt, was at last realized the practical clothing long since adopted by the other European nations for their colonial soldiers.

The officers also received, as a day uniform, the white linen jacket, to be replaced on occasion by the blue flannel dolman.

Thus it took more than twenty years to accomplish this great reform in hygienic clothing, which an ill-advised economy had postponed, to the great detriment of the health of our troops.

For the campaign in Madagascar, garments of flannel and of brown linen were adopted, the first for evening and the second for day wear. In the evening it is absolutely necessary to replace the linen by a warmer material, especially in the case of the garments which protect the stomach.

Every country may require some modifications in the clothing. In a hot country, the object of clothing, at least during the day, is to protect the body from the solar heat, while permitting its own heat to be emitted. Now, after Coulier, cotton and linen have a much greater emissive power than wool; but they absorb humidity rapidly, and the body they cover cools rapidly if it is in a perspiration. As to colors, white absorbs heat the least, black having the maximum absorbing power.

At night, absorption is no longer to be feared, and it is necessary, on the contrary, to prevent a too rapid emission of the body's heat, favored by a diminution of temperature, sometimes considerable. It is therefore necessary to change the clothing to that which will give more protection than linen and cotton and which will absorb humidity well and become cool slowly, such as light-weight woolens or flannel.

§ II. *The Different Articles of Clothing.*

From what we have just seen, clothing of white linen and white cotton will give the best results. If the white color is too easily soiled or too visible to warrant its being chosen, the choice should fall neither upon black, blue, nor even red, but should be limited to the light tints bordering upon yellow or light brown. A brown color which gets lighter when washed would seem to fulfill the conditions reasonably well. Besides, as a simple material of cotton or linen applied directly upon the tissues would cause a too rapid cooling of the body, there should be at least two layers superimposed; the first, applied directly to the skin (waistcoat, cotton drawers, shirt); the second, forming the outside clothing (paletot and trousers of linen or cotton). These two envelopes, having between them a layer of air, which is a bad conductor of heat, diminish absorption on the one hand, and a too rapid elimination of heat on the other.

The adoption of the brown linen clothing was rational, it is excellent for the hot hours of the day; it is less visible than white and is not so easily soiled. The brown linen clothing now issued to the French troops is lighter than that of the English, but the color will not resist more than two or three washings. The superiority of the English color is due to the combined use of areca nuts or of walnut husks and a salt of iron, which enables it to resist the decolorizing action of the sun and also of water, alcohol, weak acids, alkalis, and hypochlorites. In France the coloring is done with brown analine, curcuma, roucou, logwood, etc., whence the slight resistance of these colors and their incontestible inferiority.

There is a defect in the brown jacket. It is cut much too low, leaving the neck uncovered. If it is important not to compress the region of the neck, it is necessary to protect it against the sun's rays; a collar capable of being turned up and down at will might be adopted.

As underclothing, every man ought to have two shirts of cotton flannel, less irritating than the flannel waistcoats; two pairs of drawers, a belt of wool, similar to that of the Zouaves, and a belt of flannel; also, two handkerchiefs, two napkins, and a neckerchief.

The flannel pea-jacket, while natty for review, is too heavy and warm to be worn during the day, under any circumstances. Except in Tong-King in winter, it ought to be for night wear; but then it is indispensable.

The trousers are subject to the same remarks as the clothing for the trunk so far as the nature, color, and flexibility of texture are concerned. The necessity of replacing the linen, in the evening, by a material affording more protection and warmth, is still more imperious with regard to the trousers, by reason of the great sensibility of the abdominal organs and of the extreme frequence of the affections which concern them. It is necessary then to provide linen trousers for the day and flannel ones for the night.

The outside clothing, comprising the great-coat and cloak, should be provided. Useless in the hot countries, except in Tong-King in winter, they should be deposited, on the debarkation of the troops, in the store-houses at headquarters, to be obtained again at the time of returning to France. They will then be indispensable, at least at the end of the voyage, as will also be cloth trousers.

On expeditions, the impermeable covering with which the Americans have long provided their soldiers would be of more service than a cloak. If the rain surprises the column on the march, the men unroll the cover over the head and arms, turning the rubber side out. This improvised garment falling behind and slightly before, without ever masking the view, would leave the sides free for evaporation and at the same time prevent the men from getting wet.

For officers, the clothing should comprise: a pea-jacket of English flannel (blue or red), with a very low standing collar; a brown linen vest, one pair of trousers of blue flannel with stripes in piping, according to arm; and one pair of trousers of brown linen.

The best head-covering is the one which unites to stability the protection of the back of the neck and the eyes. The only head-gear admissible in the daytime is the colonial helmet, which permits the air to circulate freely around the head and to escape through the openings; the visor is lined with leather or cloth of a green color to soften the effect of reverberation.

Formerly the colonial helmet was subject to some criticisms of detail; it was too heavy; it is now much less so, and can be lightened still more. It was too narrow at the sides, and what it gained in elegance it lost in failing to protect sufficiently the sides of the head; it has been enlarged without damage to the shooting capacity of the wearer.

In campaign, with a view to obviating the too great visibility of the helmets, it is well to put on a cover with flowing ends, which increases at the same time the protection of the temples and of the nape of the neck; the best material is still the brown linen. While furnishing protection from the direct action of the sun's rays, it protects at the same time from reflection, which is the cause of numerous febrile attacks, for *fever is often taken through the eyes.* With the object of giving more effective protection to the organs of vision, the wearing of spectacles of smoked glass should be authorized on the march and on guard. The English in Egypt have used them. With the same end, the river boats used for the transport of the *personnel* should have double tents with curtains of blue bolting-cloth.

Every man found without his helmet between the rising and the setting of the sun ought to be considered guilty of disobedience of orders and severely punished. It is a necessity to prevent the soldiers from exposing themselves to the sun as well as to the nocturnal cooling.

The cap has its *raison d'être* only as a night head-covering. It should only be used between sunset and sunrise. In any place, the cap, which is a protection from neither heat nor rain and compresses the head, from which it keeps the air, ought not to be worn during the day. During the Madagascar campaign the head-dress called *bonnet de police* was preferred to the cap—and seemed much more hygienic, because it protected the eyes and ears.

The function of the *shoe* is to sustain the foot, to preserve it from sores, excoriations, and wounds which would result from marching barefoot, and to defend it from the incessant attack of innumerable enemies: serpents, fleas, chigres, scorpions, *bêtes rouges*, lice of the agouti, bloodsuckers, etc. It is evidently improper to give colonial troops light shoes of cloth, as they would have too little resistance for marching; nor could one dream of making them imitate the natives, who march barefoot.

The shoe must be both solid and flexible, and must be kept, in spite of the heat and humidity of the hot country, in such a condition that it can be easily put on and removed.

In Madagascar, the officers were provided with boots or with brodekins with legs; the men had Neapolitan brodekins for the march and a pair of *espadrilles* for repose. That was an excellent innovation; it would be desirable to have the soles of the *espadrilles* made of thick leather and very projecting. The reform might have been made complete by giving light gaiters of sheep-leather, more convenient to keep in good order than the cloth legs.

To keep the shoes of their African soldiers in a suitable condition of flexibility, the Italians recommend a mixture of fish-oil, turpentine, and grease.

Before the march, the feet should be washed with water slightly alcoholized; they should then be greased with soap, or, better still, with grease. In the absence of socks of cotton or linen, the foot should be enveloped with a strip of the latter material. At the end of the march, the men should wash their feet, using warm water when possible; the heavy shoes should then be replaced by the light ones.

A white umbrella lined with a material of green or blue is indispensable for all officers or agents obliged to superintend work in the hot hours of the day.

With regard to equipment, it will suffice to say that in colonial expeditions, a man ought to carry on his person only his arms, ammunition, some food, small articles for change, and a waterproof. The soldier on the march in the Tropics, cannot carry a weight averaging 25 kilograms without great inconvenience. Even admitting that all the equipment be of aluminum, as has been proposed, the weight would still be too heavy. This is one of the great difficulties of military expeditions in the hot countries, for it necessitates joining to the combatants a veritable army of coolies to carry the equipment.

Each soldier ought to have a coolie. The campaign in Madagascar was attended with sad results because this condition was neglected. The soldier on the march was obliged to carry his knapsack, as well as other articles of accoutrement and camp equipage. To impose so heavy a burden upon a European in the hot countries is to condemn him to inevitable sickness.

§ III. Maintenance of Clothing.

In the chief places of the colonies and at posts easy of access, the troops receive regularly, as in France, the clothing and linen allowed by the regulations.

It is not so in the case of isolated posts. Difficult even in ordinary times, the supply of clothing to meet all demands then becomes a problem.

In the Soudan, for example, after seven or eight months of work, the men relieving the garrisons of the posts arrived there with clothing in tatters and incapable of the function assigned it by hygienic principles.

The means of remedying this situation, so defective and prejudicial to health, would be to have in the storehouses of these posts a sufficient quantity of clothing to properly supply the men, instead of compelling them to remain for months with nothing to cover them but uniforms in rags or other unsuitable clothing.

The washing of the linen is important. In the cities it can be done by contract, and a laundry would be an advantage at every post. The men would then be able to take care of their linen without exposing themselves, either on the river banks or under unhygienic shelters, to the emanations from the shore or to the action of solar reverberation. They would also be freed from the services of the exotic washerwomen, who tear the linen and often return it only half clean.

In taking care of the clothing, the linen, and the various articles of equipment, the question of cleanliness is connected with another, of even greater importance, which should be understood, not only by the doctors, but also by the officers; this is the question of disinfection, especially the disinfection of articles in use.

The disinfection of clothing and bedding is a measure

which should be taken in all colonial garrisons in case of death and also in contagious diseases, after the soldiers are cured. This would prevent many cases of disease and death from the reviviscence of the morbid germs contained in the effects.

In large centers, provided with improved appliances, the clothing and bedding are placed in a drying stove, receiving vapor, under pressure, at 110 to 115 degrees.

Where these large apparatus are not available, a solution of bichloride of mercury of 1:1000 can be used, in which the clothing and bedding are dipped; they are then placed in boiling water, except such articles as would be injured.

Clothing is often the means of propagating epidemic diseases, and articles of clothing which have been worn should never be issued without first subjecting them to effective disinfection.

CHAPTER IV.

MILITARY LIFE.

No one is ignorant that in the Tropics the days and nights are of practically equal length. The first hours of the day are undoubtedly the most healthful, and if it is not a good thing, especially in a paludal country, to get up before sunrise, it is not bad to rise with the sun. From six to ten o'clock in the morning is the first working period of colonial life; the second extends from three to seven in the afternoon. One does not go out at all from noon to four o'clock, and during this time affairs are practically suspended. There is a reason for these habits in the colonies. It is dangerous to be exposed to the sun at the zenith, and the European soldier, more sensitive than the native, should be warned against the dangers he may be made to run by a hygienic error. The military authority, always vigilant, will be able to protect him by establishing a list of service, which alternates work and rest and takes into account the exigencies of climate.

§ 1. *Occupations of the Soldier.*

In the colonies, drills are necessary to occupy the men, to prevent them from losing the profit of the military instruction received in France, and to prepare them for the eventualities of an expedition; they are also beneficial to health and are a precious antidote to *ennui*.

They should invariably fulfill a double condition:
1. Take place at selected hours.
2. Be of short duration.

The hour naturally indicated is the morning hour following rising. It is usually preferred, as being the most agreeable and the one in which the man is in best condition and best capable of effort.

With reveille, about five o'clock, according to place and season, the man goes to drill, either every day, or two or three times a week, from six to seven o'clock. The drill lasts from one to two hours. The men should never be sent to drill, however, on mornings when there is a thick fog. Experience and observation show that such fogs, rising with the sun, are the surest vehicles of the parasite of malaria. An imprudence would also be committed by ever sending the men to drill on an empty stomach; the first breakfast should precede the drill, as an empty stomach predisposes the system to the pernicious influence of emanations from the ground.

Under these conditions, in all the colonies, the soldier can be exercised for at least an hour in the manual of arms and in various movements, with rests of five minutes at the end of each half-hour. When the men are well trained, it will be advisable to reduce the length of the drills, which are more enervating in the hot countries than in Europe, when they are prolonged or too often repeated.

Marches should be of short duration. As it is necessary to prepare the men, even by a little training, for a mobilization, which might take place at any time, it would be well to make them execute, once a week in the good season, and from six to nine o'clock in the morning, a march of fifteen kilometers, during which care should be taken to observe all the precautions taken in time of war. We will take occasion to refer to this matter again in the chapter on expeditions.

It is evident that longer marches will be required in actual service and that there will not always be latitude to halt ten minutes every hour; but under pretext of training, exhausting effort should never be uselessly exacted. A company accustomed to make a march of fifteen kilometers frequently, and without inconvenience, can make double the distance on occasion, under the influence of a moral stimulant, especially if it is vigorously commanded. The colonial, like the metropolitan soldier, will do his duty when it is a question of getting at the enemy, of marching to the sound of cannon, of flying to the aid of a place or of his brothers in arms. Although in France it is permissible for a commanding officer to test the resisting powers of his men by one or two practice marches, the fatigue of which will affect their health only slightly, it is not the same in the hot countries. Experience of what takes place on expeditions proves that an exercise of this nature may have disastrous consequences for a company.

The reviews should also take place in the morning at the same hour prescribed for drill. Not being fatigued by a day of heat and occupations, the men will present a more cheerful and alert appearance.

From ten o'clock in the morning to four in the evening, all outside drills should be prohibited.

In this interval, gymnastics may be tolerated. A light costume should be worn, there should be a sufficiently long rest between movements, more diversity and less monotony should be sought, and, above all, there should be great latitude concerning the number and difficulty of the exercises to be practiced.

It is the same with fencing, which should be carried on indoors.

In addition to physical military exercises, the profession of arms includes theoretical instruction. This should be given upon the galleries instead of in the rooms, unless special places are available, such as dining-rooms, school-rooms, etc.

The best hours will be from eight to ten in the morning and from two to four in the afternoon.

Theoretical instruction should never be too much prolonged under penalty of tiring the soldier, who ends by succumbing to the heat, joined to the immobility, and loses all the benefit of the instruction. An hour's duration should suffice.

The hours suitable for theoretical military instruction are also suitable for general instruction.

There is no objection to devoting an hour a day, upon an average, to lessons in reading, writing, and arithmetic. For men more advanced, the instruction in the barracks can and should be extended so as to become a regular course for adults.

Above all, an attempt should be made to interest the soldier; that is to say, to teach him about all that surrounds him, to make him acquainted with the colony in which he lives, its resources and its products. This elementary instruction should be given by officers, assisted by non-commissioned officers, and the post surgeon could add with profit some lectures upon the special hygiene of the climate. This teaching should be in the nature of object lessons and adapted to those who receive it. Through them it will be spread and will give an exact knowledge of our possessions beyond the seas. The military service will then have the double advantage of providing our colonial empire not only with defenders in the present, but also with arms for the future.

The officers and non-commissioned officers on their part should often devote themselves to work, either to cheat *ennui*, or to instruct themselves, to prepare for examinations or for the military schools. They should know, however, that an excess of mental work is dangerous and that the expenditure of strength is quite as considerable as that produced by physical work. The hours to choose are those of the morning, or at least of the forenoon, to the exclusion of the hottest portions of the day. As to night work, it ought to be absolutely interdicted, or at least should never encroach on the hours which should be devoted to sleep.

§ II. *Fatigue Duty and Other Work.*

It will no longer be possible to see sailors coaling their ship at the hour when the convicts are taking their *siesta*, as once came to pass in Guiana. There are fatigue duties which must be done by the soldier; but he ought to be exempt from certain kinds of work; in any case, soldiers ought not to be transformed into coolies.

FATIGUE.

There is a distinction to be established between the fatigue duties on the interior of the buildings and those outside.

Interior Fatigue.—The soldier ought to be charged with the care of his quarters, his bed, and his clothing; in all that concerns the sweeping, good order, cleanliness, and regular disinfection of the buildings, he will never be better served than by himself.

Doctor Reynaud gives some excellent advice on this subject:

"Immediately after the men rise, open the windows and the blinds of the gallery on the sunny side, leave the beds uncovered for a few moments, pass slightly dampened cloths over the floor, and let it dry immediately for sweeping; require the men to brush and polish their effects on the gallery, then sweep it and wash it with a damp mop, or even flood it with water if it is covered with glazed tiles and has sufficient slope to insure drainage; once a week, wipe the panes of doors and windows. The same day, it will be well to add to the water used to wet the cleaning-cloths a certain quantity of carbolized water, of say 50:1000, or a solution of bichloride of mercury. The dust collected in the interstices and corners should also be sterilized."

The cleanliness of the rooms and of their materials includes also the care of the bedding. The sheets should be washed once a month at least, and the coverings aired and beaten on the galleries. Ordinary mattresses, unless those of cocoa hair or granulated cork are alone used, should be renovated and beaten once a year in ordinary times. It is also necessary to provide for the painting of the rooms, the coating of the feet of the beds with petroleum or carbolized tar, the beating and repairing of the mosquito bars, the insufflations of chamomile powder, and the distribution of the cuspidors, disinfected with a sulphate of copper solution of 50:1000 or with whitewash.

There are also soldiers, designated by roster, who are charged with allowing no unclean thing to remain in the quarters. Through their care, the sweepings and the *débris* of the tables after each meal are collected and placed in the dirt-boxes; the utensils are cleaned, being washed in warm water every time they are used.

Exterior Fatigue.—The policing of the annexes or of the yards of the barracks should never be done by whites, as much for hygienic reasons as to inspire respect for the uniform on the part of the natives. Under the supervision of Europeans, there are coolies or laborers who can always perform, in the English fashion, the service of cleaning the yards, prisons, store-houses, and, with more reason, the latrines and other sinks. After the moveable *tinettes* are taken outside and away from the barracks, it belongs to the coolies alone to flood them and wash them clean with disinfecting solutions.

If certain interior fatigue duties are harassing to the French soldier, what is to be said of the purely exterior fatigue? Here, it is necessary to go for water, every day, several kilometers from the barracks; there, the port of debarkation, which supplies the post, is separated from it by a long and tiresome route, over which must be drawn or carried boxes, packages, and casks, which sometimes have to be hoisted to quite a height at the military buildings. Moreover, it is a laborious and often perilous task, which requires a large portion of the effective force, at dates often close together, either to go to a distant roadstead to disembark the provisions from a vessel, or to go there to bring back the material. The wood details to the neighboring forests, the extraction of stone from a quarry, and the procuring of sand for the gardens, are always prejudicial to the health of Europeans. How many attacks of fever or of dysentery have had their origin in fatigue duty of this description!

Thus, every garrison should always have native coolies, who, under the supervision of Europeans, are charged with all troublesome fatigue both on the interior and exterior of the military buildings. At the rate of one coolie to ten men, all would go smoothly. The savings realized upon days in the hospital and medicines from the infirmary would provide for their maintenance without increase of expense for the regiment. Moreover, in many of the colonies, the local administrations employ a certain number of prisoners on road and gardening works. Why should the military service not profit by this manual labor as well as the municipality?

In the penitentiary colonies, without mixing the penal and military element, certain exterior work could be done by the convicts. If foreign manual labor should fail, it would be necessary to provide wagons, carts, horses, oxen, and mules to accomplish the cartage and transport.

WORK.

In addition to fatigue duties, there is other work about the barracks and military buildings, which must be considered. For example, gardening, working at a trade, and works of excavation and defense.

Gardening.—The maintenance of a garden plays an important part in the military life of a garrison, for on it largely depends the welfare of the company and the officers from an alimentary standpoint. The officers and soldiers are usually eager to give great care to the cultivation of the garden.

The gardener sometimes lives in the garden, in a sort of hut of primitive construction. While there is no serious inconvenience in this in certain colonies, it would not be safe in a paludal country. The guardian of the garden at night should be a native. Digging, removing the earth, and other laborious work should likewise be performed by native coolies serving as permanent aids to the European gardener, whose active duty should be limited to direction and supervision. The sowing, gathering of fruits, harvesting of vegetables, and sprinkling might sometimes be done, without inconvenience, by Europeans selected from men undergoing punishment or from volunteers. They should work only morning and evening, never during the hours when outside work is forbidden.

Working at a Trade.—This kind of work, as performed by soldiers in the colonies, is of several kinds.

There are first the sedentary trades, those of the tailor, shoemaker, hair-dresser, armorer, painter, which are not fatiguing and are carried on in a desultory way.

It is often necessary to call upon the special talents of the men, who are generally satisfied to occupy their leisure in utilizing their knowledge.

Certain trades which are more fatiguing, as those of butcher, baker, and cook, should only be practiced by European professionals. They should always be assisted by a sufficient number of native coolies to exempt their function from all laborious and humiliating work.

In addition to these interior works, there are others which arise unexpectedly and which it is incumbent on the professional military mechanics to perform: soldiers of engineers, pontoniers, and artillery mechanics. Sometimes there is an insufficient number of these professionals and they have to be assisted by soldiers taken as far as possible from those who were masons, carpenters, joiners, or slaters before their entry into the service, for it is a question in this case of the construction or repair of military buildings.

This work ought to be done during the hours chosen for outdoor drills—that is to say, in the morning or evening. In the hottest hours, about noon, work should be entirely suspended, even in the buildings or under the more or less improvised sheds. There, the time prescribed for exterior work might occasionally be extended an hour or two, morning and evening. In unhealthy countries, all work of this kind is most troublesome and dangerous, as it exposes Europeans to the sun and to febrile emanations.'

In 1840, Thévenot had already pointed out the exceptional morbidity and mortality among the artillerymen and mechanics, especially during expeditions and during the early periods of occupation of a post. He attributed this, with reason, to the special works on which these soldiers were then employed. Observations of the same nature have since been made in the Soudan, Dahomey, and again, but recently, in Madagascar. At Koutonou, in 1890, the mechanics of artillery employed in erecting barracks showed a morbidity of 61 per cent. after a stay of three months.

These workmen should be subjected to all the more careful supervision because many of them who are sick avoid presenting themselves to the medical officer in order not to be deprived of the high pay accorded them. This is an important consideration. If it were disregarded, and the small number of exemptions furnished by the workmen taken as a basis, the conclusion might be reached that active work in insalubrious regions has a good influence and is even necessary for the health. It is also true that high pay often leads to excesses of all kinds on the part of those who draw it. It is the duty of commanding officers to prevent this by allowing the soldiers only a part of the sums earned. The balance of the money should be deposited in the corps-chest and paid the men at the end of their colonial service, unless those interested prefer to send the amount of their savings to France.

Works of Excavation and Defense require a greater expenditure of energy, are always executed on the exterior, and in paludal countries have the additional disadvantage of exposing the soldier directly to the emanations from the soil. In this respect there is a considerable difference between low and marshy countries like those of Indo-China, the West Coast of Africa, and the littoral of Madagascar, and dry or elevated countries like the high plateaux of the Antilles, or the coralline and permeable soils of the oceanic islands.

Dutrouleau observed long ago, and after General Douzelot, that work in healthy places, even during the warm hours, was beneficial to health. The fortifications constructed in the volcanic formations of Guadeloupe and Martinique, in 1840 and the following years, had no other effect than to improve the health of the troops. It was the same, later, when Camp Jacob was established. The fact is easily proved. The *fusiliers de discipline* in service in the Saints and in Martinique, although engaged in laborious works, have had only four deaths in five years out of an average effective strength of 168 per year. This percentage is nine times less than in the *infanterie de marine* stationed in all our colonial possessions.

During the first years of our occupation of New Caledonia, our soldiers were also obliged to construct numerous earth-works and roads—at Noumea and in that vicinity. Nevertheless the sanitary condition remained excellent.

Passing from the Antilles and Oceanica to our colonies in Indo-China, Guiana, Senegal, the Soudan, Dahomey, and Madagascar, to those, in a word, which have long had a bad reputation, too often verified, as *fever countries*, we can prove the grievous influence exercised upon the health of troops by the handling of alluvial soil.

In Guiana, in 1763, 12,000 soldiers and colonists sent from France attempted the cultivation of the land. They were soon reduced from 12,000 to 2,000.

Druing the first years of the conquest of Cochin-China, at a time when no military expeditions were in progress, the military and other works undertaken by the troops entailed a mortality of 115 per 1000, in a corps of 3,600 men. More recently, in Tong-King, hundreds of deaths have occurred among the men employed on the defensive works at Phu-ly, Phulang-Tuong, Lang-Kep, Chû, etc.

In 1840, during the little expedition which led to the occupation of Nossi-Bé, there were a few earth-works to establish. There was such a recrudescence of fevers that 80 men were lost in a very short time. The deplorable results of the attempts made by the whites to handle the virgin soil of Madagascar are known only too well.

"Who moves the soil in a paludal country," said Lind, two hundred years ago, "digs there his grave." It has been proved by experience that Europeans can perform laborious tasks under any meteorological conditions provided they are protected from the influence of the soil. This was the case with the sailors of the Madagascar flotilla, who, in 1885, and again in 1895, led the roughest sort of life on the river gunboats and at Tamatave and Majunga. The mortality was much less among these sailors than among the soldiers living on the land.

In paludal countries the European cannot work the soil; native coolies should be exclusively used in the construction of earth-works, and only the want of manual labor justifies the use, with discretion, of the native troops. It should never be forgotten that no race is absolutely immune to paludism.

The opening of the famous canal joining Chandoc to the Gulf of Siam would formerly have cost the lives of 80,000 Annamites.

The Panama Railroad has seen as many Chinese die as there are ties in its road-bed. Bear in mind also the mortality among the Marocains in the Haut-Fleuve at the time of our first campaigns in the Soudan.

The conclusion is that in hot countries, especially paludal countries, reservation must be used in the measure of fatigue to impose upon white troops, and even upon native troops, if their health is to be preserved. But it does not follow that they should be left unoccupied and inactive. The ability of the commander will be shown by keeping his troops constantly in good condition without exhausting their strength. Even in times of epidemic it would be a great mistake to allow the men to abandon themselves completely to idleness and *ennui*, anxious for the morrow and consumed by inquietude. From *ennui* and inactivity to the complete loss of the appetite is only a step, and when the appetite is gone, disease is near at hand.

As for earth-works, it must be known when to put a stop to them, in war as well as in peace, since it is a fact that in paludal countries their influence has been more fatal to the troops than the most murderous epidemics.

It is a long time since the habit was renounced of allowing colonial soldiers to work for the inhabitants. From the standpoints of health, morality, and discipline, this measure can only be applauded. The working of the ground was above all the most pernicious and naturally the most in demand. It would be veritable folly to go back to such a system, and it would be less excusable to do so in our time, as it is impossible to plead ignorance of the dangers incurred.

§ III. *Bathing.*

In the Tropics, especially after work, as much to rid the skin of the products accumulated by perspiration as to carry off a certain amount of heat, the bath is at once a necessity and a benefit. It enables a man to struggle with advantage against the numerous eruptions which overrun the skin.

Under the forms of douches, baths, immersions, and sprinklings, the men ought to find in every post the means of giving themselves total ablutions daily.

In France, recourse is had to the Haro process, which can be easily and cheaply placed in the smallest barracks. It furnishes douches for the men at very small expense. By means of a suction and force-pump furnished with a nozzle or sprinkling-head, the soldiers are sprinkled with a mixture of hot and cold water. The fire-pump, in the colonial posts, is entirely adapted for this use and also for filling the reservoirs and apparatus of the douche.

It is in the morning, between nine and ten o'clock, before the second breakfast and after the hours of exterior service, that the men, in groups, should present themselves at the douche and at the pool. With the approval of the medical authority and the commandant, especially at certain epochs, a second hydropathic seance might be held at five o'clock in the evening. These seances should be short, only a few minutes; they should not be obligatory unless demanded for cleanliness. It would even be proper to forbid the douches and cold sprinkling to soldiers recently attacked by diarrhœa or suffering from intermittent fever. For a subject in these conditions, or even one ill-disposed from paludal causes, a douche or a cold bath would suffice to produce a return of the attack.

Hot or cold baths in bath-tubs are not in fashion in the barracks, outside the infirmaries; the same may be said of sea and river baths, in spite of their advantages as exercise and as a stimulant to the system. In the colonies they are either not very practicable or dangerous: not very practicable when the price is a long walk; dangerous on account of the sun, the crocodiles, the sharks, and a thousand noxious fish, none the less to be avoided because less formidable.

It is already known how frequent are the deaths by drowning among our colonial soldiers. There is a veritable danger in permitting men to bathe alone. More than any where else, they should be positively forbidden to do so in the hot countries.

§ IV. *Amusements and Rest.*

To preserve among our soldiers of the colonial army the health of the mind, which is as indispensable as the health of the body, it is necessary to provide them in the barracks with all the distractions compatible with the profession of arms and the exigencies of discipline.

One of the first things deserving favorable consideration is the establishment in all the posts of little libraries. With good will, the money could be found, even by appeal to the liberality of the officers, non-commissioned officers, and colonists, and, above all, to the aid societies.

To the libraries should be added a few games of dominos, checkers, and loto. The ideal would be the union of these various attractions in a special room, which would become a sort of club for the men, advantageously replacing the existing canteens. There, each one would be at perfect liberty to rest, read, amuse himself with the various games, and attend to his correspondence. Reading-rooms have been installed in certain barracks in France, but it is in the English and Dutch colonies that models of this kind are found. In Java, for example, the canteen is a very airy place, situated in a large garden provided with the various games which the soldiers love—bowling, lawn-tennis, etc. There is also a billiard-table; theatricals, always so pleasing to the soldier, concerts, and even balls, are encouraged there. It is the only place where the Dutch soldier can get spirituous drinks, and he is allowed to get only a very small quantity; in return, he obtains tea, coffee, and lemonade *ad libitum* and at a very low price.

It may seem difficult for us to create institutions of this nature on account of our customs and of the protection afforded local commerce in our colonies; all military commanders have at least the right to try it in the inclosure of the barracks. The end to be attained is to draw the soldiers from the allurements of the saloon and to seek to amuse them while preserving their health.

Rest in the colonies should be taken in two installments: one at night, the other in the daytime.

The latter, the *siesta*, has its partisans and its detractors. Still, as far as concerns the soldier, rising at five o'clock, doing guard duty at night and attending drills during the morning, a little rest or even sleep is a necessity about midday. It is not only absolutely harmless, but, practiced with discretion, the *siesta* can have only a favorable influence upon the health.

As for rest at night, its duration can never be abridged without inconvenience. For this reason, nocturnal exercises should be extremely limited. Night marches, unless demanded by a superior interest, should be proscribed.

CHAPTER V.

MEDICAL SERVICE.

To anticipate diseases by appropriate measures is not sufficient; the development must be opposed and the gravity appeased by giving the most careful attention to the sick. This is accomplished by a judicious organization of the medical service.

§ I. *Medical Personnel.*

The *personnel* distributed in each colony ought to be sufficient to assure the working of the entire military medical service. The proportions should be based not only upon the effective strength, but also upon the number of posts, the grouping or dissemination of the troops, and the difficulty of communications between the different posts.

Medical Officers.—The number of officers of the Medical Department should be great enough to permit the assignment of one wherever there is an isolated group of at least 60 men.

In France, an infantry regiment of three battalions, united or scattered in two or three garrisons, includes: 1 surgeon of the 1st class (*médecin principal de la Marine*); 1 surgeon of the 2d class (*médecin de 1re classe de la Marine*); 2 assistant surgeons (*médecin de 2e classe de la Marine*); making 4. In time of war this number is raised to 6.

In the colonies there are often less than four surgeons to the regiment, whatever its strength. Moreover, the native regiments never have a chief surgeon—that is to say, an officer of superior rank. The method of assigning medical officers is quite different from that in France; nevertheless, the service in the colonies is very important and the decisions to be made demand more promptness, more experience, maturity, and authority on the part of officers of the Medical Department.

It is especially to be regretted that at the posts of the interior an isolated European or native company is often found without any surgeon at all. In these cases, medical attendance is given by the colonial surgeon of the district or of a neighboring district, or even by an assistant surgeon, attached to a post sometimes very remote, who comes once or twice a month or weekly. In time of peace this system has the disadvantage of failing to give the men prompt and sufficient attention. In case the surgeon belongs to the colonial service and is therefore ignorant of the regimental service, it has the inconvenience of placing the medical action outside the control of the commanding officer. In time of expedition (the permanent condition in certain regions), when the garrison of one of these posts is mobilized, it is in danger, if operating alone, of having no surgeon to follow it and of failing to meet one during part of the operations.

It has often been proved that the medical *personnel* is insufficient for its task, the result being a very high death-rate, due to the absence of sanitary measures and medical assistance.

Thus, in Tong-King, in 1888, there were 678 deaths; in 1889, 382 out of 1069; and in 1890, 286 out of 1125. These were the results of the above conditions.

In order to furnish all soldiers with the medical assistance to which they are entitled, it is necessary to increase the number of surgeons with troops.

With the object of fixing the ideas upon this point and of demonstrating the urgent necessity of reform, we give a table showing the medical officers attached to the infantry and artillery of Marine on January 1, 1898.

Lists of Surgeons for Duty with Troops.

France.

	Chief Surgeons.	Surgeons of the 1st Class.	Surgeons of the 2d Class.	Total.
Artillery.				
1st Regiment	1	3	3	7
2d Regiment	1	1	1	3
Companies of Mechanics			2	2
Pyrotechnic School		1	2	3
Infantry.				
1st Regiment	1	1	2	4
2d Regiment	1	1	2	4
3d Regiment	1	1	3	5
4th Regiment	1	2	3	6
5th Regiment	1	1	1	3
6th Regiment	1	1	3	5
7th Regiment	1	1	2	4
8th Regiment	1	1	3	5
Paris Battalion	1	2	1	4
Detachments in Crete		2	2	4
Total	11	18	20	59

Colonies.

	Chief Surgeons.	Surgeons of the 1st Class.	Surgeons of the 2d Class.	Total.
European Troops.				
9th Regiment	1		2	3
10th Regiment	1		2	3
11th Regiment		1	1	2
12th Regiment			3	3
13th Regiment	1	3	4	8
Battalion of Martinique			1	1
Battalion of Guiana		1	2	3
Battalion of Senegal			1	1
Battalion of Reunion		1		1
Total	3	6	16	25
Native Troops.				
Annamite Tirailleurs		3	1	4
Tong-King Tirailleurs		5	15	20
Soudan Tirailleurs		1	3	4
Senegal Tirailleurs		1	2	3
Houssa Tirailleurs		1	1	2
Total		11	22	33
Grand Total	3	17	38	58

We find a total of 117 surgeons, 59 in France and 58 in the colonies.

In France, the 59 surgeons attached to the troops are sufficient for the needs of the service, inasmuch as the vacancies caused by departures to the colonies are immediately filled by surgeons from the general list of the Marine; these last, selected by roster, serve at least two years in the regiments.

In the colonies, 58 surgeons, from which number must be deducted those who are sick, on leave, or changing station, have to suffice for the regimental service of 14,000 Europeans and 25,000 natives, or a total of 39,000 men, scattered by battalions and companies, always in movement, often in war. The Europeans have barely 25 surgeons—that is to say, less than 2 per 1000 men; the natives, with only 33 for 25,000 men, are still less favored.

It is not possible to demand too strongly:

1. An increase of the number of medical officers.
2. An augmentation in the number of superior officers to direct the service.

There might be adopted for each 3 battalions of 4 companies the following: 1 chief surgeon, 2 surgeons of the 1st class, and 3 surgeons of the 2d class; total, 6.

The distribution could be made thus:

1. In each regiment of 3 battalions, 1 principal surgeon as chief, with the senior surgeon of the 1st class ready to replace him.
2. In each regiment of 2 battalions, or in the case of 2 battalions combined, a surgeon of the 1st class.
3. In each regiment of 3 battalions, 3 surgeons of the 2d class; and for each regiment of 2 battalions, 2 surgeons of the 2d class.

The number of surgeons of the 2d class could be varied

according to colony; it should be based upon the number of posts to be supplied and the condition of the country occupied. It could be reduced in Reunion, the Antilles, and Guiana; in Indo-China, on the Coast of Africa, and in New Caledonia, it should be the regulation number; in Madagascar and the Soudan, it should always be increased.

The number of surgeons necessary for regimental service in the colonies, in our opinion, is as follows:

FOR SERVICE WITH TROOPS IN THE COLONIES.

Chief Surgeons	4	For
Surgeons of the 1st Class	13	European
Surgeons of the 2d Class	19	Troops.
Total	36	
Chief Surgeons	6	For
Surgeons of the 1st Class	14	Native
Surgeons of the 2d Class	22	Troops.
Total	42	

This would be an increase of 20, certainly not excessive. It would give 2 surgeons per 1000 men, and we know that in France, in time of war, there are officers of the Medical Department to a mobilized regiment forming a group of 3000 men.

Moreover, the regimental surgeons would everywhere insure the medical care of their soldiers in the wards of the colonial hospitals transformed into mixed hospitals, as in France.

The advantages which would result for the men, for the administration, and also for the Treasury, would be very appreciable. Actually the daily hospital charges in the French colonies have been 13 fr. 60 for officers and 9 fr. 14 for the men, against an average of 4 fr. 10 in the foreign ports.

In connection with colonial expeditions, we shall have occasion to speak of the number of surgeons to be provided for the performance of duties outside of those directly connected with the troops—viz., in the field hospitals, on transports and hospital-ships, at sanitaria, and, in a word, all duties connected with sanitary measures.

Nurses.—The number of nurses with the colonial troops should also be increased. In France and in the colonies, each European regiment has a *regimental nurse* from each battalion, chosen from the most capable and best instructed of the auxiliary nurses. Unfortunately, the native regiments are too often unprovided with them. The auxiliaries among these troops are rather coolies than nurses. However, Europeans or natives, regimental nurses or auxiliary nurses, they are not *professionals*, but are only *improvised*. Now a nurse can no more be improvised than a surgeon.

In the short term of service there is not time to teach them enough to enable them to perform their delicate functions. Among the auxiliaries are found some who are very useful as bearers or hospital attendants, but there are scarcely ever professional nurses. Now, in the colonies, especially, the surgeons, often isolated, need excellent assistants, capable of training and directing a certain number of natives. The Annamites and the natives of Tong-King make excellent hospital nurses when they have had the necessary practice. There should be, then, in the colonial army, a corps of nurses like the corps of surgeons—that is to say, a corps of *professionals*. This body should include adjutants, sergeant-majors, sergeants, corporals, and nurses of 1st and 2d classes.

Nurses of the grades of adjutant and sergeant-major could be detached to the small posts without a surgeon, and could render the greatest service in such a case.

There should be 1 sergeant per regiment, 1 corporal per battalion, and 1 nurse per company.

In a column, these non-commissioned officers, with the

auxiliaries and the bearers, would form, under direction of the surgeon, a sanitary *personnel* equal to all exigencies. The organization of the nurses of the fleet serves as an example: the non-commissioned officers, who are professional nurses, are assigned alone to small vessels, such as the torpedo despatch-boats, and the service is efficient. As for ships provided with a medical officer, they always have a suitable number of instructed and zealous nurses, precious auxiliaries of the medical service either afloat or ashore, in case of debarkation.

§ II. *Hospitals and Infirmaries.*

In the great centers, the colonial hospitals of to-day are fairly comfortable. Like the barracks and other military constructions, they might be classified: good or indifferent, as quarters, in our possessions the least badly provided; insufficient in certain respects; sometimes defective.

All the criticisms made in regard to the colonial barracks might be repeated as to the old hospitals; it is proper, however, to acknowledge that real progress has been made in construction. As for the installation and interior management of the wards, the regulations governing the cleanliness and salubrity of the hospital establishments in France are applicable to the colonies.

It must be added, however, that in the colonies, more than anywhere else, care should be taken to provide:

1. A system for the prevention of illicit communications between patients and the exterior.
2. Special wards for dysenteries.
3. Pavilions for contagious diseases.
4. Rooms for the insane.
5. Special vehicles and litters for transporting the patients.

We do not dwell upon disinfection appliances. While they pertain to the city, they naturally find their place in the hospital, where they could be kept, and placed at the disposition of the representative of the council of hygiene in case of need. Several of our large hospitals are provided with them.

If the colonial cities are generally sufficiently favored with respect to hospitals, it is not the same with the smaller places and the military posts. Hospitals are still found of ancient creation which have not even a room set apart for the care of the sick; others are better off in this respect, but in New Caledonia, for example, the infirmary contains only a few troop beds, and is without chair, table, cupboard—anything, in a word, which can recall its special destination. Without exacting luxurious and complicated furnishings, there should always be a *regimental infirmary*, suitable to the size of the garrison, whenever the large colonial hospitals are not in proximity to the barracks. This should also be the case in posts which have no small hospital annexed to the quarters, such as is often seen in Tong-King and Cochin-China.

A regimental infirmary, says Doctor Gayet, ought to be separated from the barracks by a yard, and should be far from noise and odors. It should always be of more than one story.

The ground floor should comprise:

1. The quarters of the non-commissioned officer in charge of the infirmary.
2. A waiting room or large hall with benches for the fatigued and lame men.
3. An examination-room, with cupboards containing the instruments, medicines, and records.
4. The office of the surgeon.
5. A store-room for the effects of the sick, the utensils, and the supplies of the infirmary.

6. A bath-room with tubs and douches.

On the second floor, there should be five wards, as follows:

1. A ward for fever patients.
2. A ward for the wounded.
3. A ward for venereal diseases.
4. A ward for non-commissioned officers.
5. A ward for convalescents.

According to the same author, the number of beds should be 3 to each 100 of the effective strength. This number may suffice if it be made to apply strictly to the sick, and the convalescents and those under treatment for venereal diseases sleep in ordinary troop beds. Such an infirmary should exist only at posts of a certain importance, garrisoned by several companies. In posts garrisoned by less than a hundred men, a simpler place, with two or three beds, a table, an armchair, chairs, and bath, would suffice. It would be well if all our small garrisons were so provided.

In case of contagious disease, one or more huts can be erected in which to care for the sick. They should afterwards be burned.

§ III. *Matériel of the Medical Department.*

The infirmaries and field hospitals of the colonial posts are not, as in France, in the neighborhood of the hospitals proper. They receive, moreover, a great number of serious cases. It may even happen that the difficulty of communications will oblige the surgeon to keep such patients there a long time. In short, these small hospitals often have to be used in the same way as the hospitals of ships. Now the war-ship, however small its tonnage, and even when it remains near the coasts, has its medical *matériel* provided and its service organized. The surgeon possesses personally a surgeon's case, which a monthly allowance enables him to maintain. There is a pharmacy aboard, with apparatus, medicines, and materials for dressings, appropriate to the effective strength embarked. All is foreseen: the furniture of the hospital, the special food for the sick, a field-chest for first aid to the wounded, a disembarkation-bag, and litters specially adapted to medical or surgical needs in case of disembarkation. The ships are no more deprived of medicine than of ammunition, and the first-aid chest is always on hand.

Why should the posts in the colonies be deprived of anything that is necessary? The instruments are kept in a box, which is often in bad condition. The medicines and dressing materials are often insufficient in quantity. Many of the small posts are even denuded of all means of assistance. Why not put the surgeon at such a place in the same situation as the surgeon afloat? Why not devise, for each colonial post, a supply-type of medicines and dressing materials, analogous to that of the ships?

There might be adopted, in addition to the main supplies, a series of 4 chests:

No. 1, for posts of 10 men, or under.
No. 2, for posts of 10 to 20 men.
No. 3, for posts of 20 to 40 men.
No. 4, for posts of 40 to 60 men.

The model of those to be kept in store-rooms of colonial hospitals could approximate to the one adopted by the Departments of War and Marine for the supply of forts and batteries in case of mobilization. These chests are always prepared in advance and kept in the store-rooms. In each newly created post there should be one or more chests, according to the strength of garrison, to be replaced at a fixed date or when there is need, the empty chests being returned to the *dépôt*. This system has been praised for the supply of ships; it would be of the greatest service in the colonies.

These medicine-chests should be a part of the fixed *matériel*, distinct from the *matériel* of mobilization, in paniers, which should also be supplied, as we shall say later on.

It is also necessary to supply for each infirmary or field hospital in the colonies:

1. One or more filters.
2. An ice-machine.
3. Some cooking utensils.
4. Litters or hand-barrows of the style of the country.
5. In certain places a small boat for the transportation and evacuation of the sick.
6. A very clear manual of instruction in first aid for sick and wounded.

In 1886, during the period of the conquest of Tong-King, the medical director of the expeditionary corps, M. Dujardin-Beaumetz, prepared, for the use of military posts without a surgeon, a clear and concise medical manual, which corresponded perfectly to the needs of the moment. Recent works contain similar and more detailed instructions.

§ IV. *Repatriation of the Sick.*

To repatriate the sick, special ships are required. The ordinary ships of war, the ships of commerce most rapid and best furnished for carrying healthy persons, do not often fulfill the requisite conditions for the sick. The periods of return have not always been judiciously chosen, at least in normal times.

HOSPITAL-TRANSPORTS.

For many long years the repatriation of the sick was accomplished in a deplorable manner.

Before 1840, in Senegal, unfortunate convalescents were

crowded upon incumbered sailing vessels, often infected with yellow fever, without suitable food, without medicines, sometimes without doctors; they returned to France not by the shortest route, *but by way of the Antilles and Guiana.*

Later, during the campaign in China, in 1860, ships of war a little better managed, the *Vengeance*, the *Dryade*, the *Garonne*, carried out troops and brought back the sick. It was the same during the campaign in Mexico. The large sailers, the *Tage*, the *Navarin*, etc., converted into transports, have long performed the service between France and New Caledonia. The last types used for this purpose, the *Magellan*, the *Calédonien*, were better adapted and more appropriate to their special service. They were large sailers, furnished with a little engine to be used in calms. Their maritime existence was ephemeral; as hospital-transports, moreover, their service would have been much restricted for want of the sick.

At the beginning of our occupation of Cochin-China, the *Orne*, the *Creuse*, and the *Sarthe* marked serious progress; and yet, although sufficient for well troops, they were not adapted for the repatriation of the sick.

It was not until November 20, 1877, that there started from Toulon the first type of the veritable hospital-transport, the *Annamite*, measuring 105 meters in length, gauging 3100 tons, and possessing an engine of 650 horse-power. Five transports of the same type, the *Tong-King*, *Mytho*, *Shamrock*, *Bien-Hoa*, and *Vinh-Long*, were successively constructed at La Seyne. The *Gironde* and the *Nive*, constructed a little later, were fitted up to transport cavalry.

These eight ships, all of iron, except the *Annamite*, were perfectly adapted to the transportation of the sick. The upper broadside could accommodate 150 bed-ridden patients, and the lower one 300 convalescents. The system of bedding was good; the ventilation easy, thanks to a system of double partitions and to horizontal wind sails, windowed at intervals and closed by grooved obturators.

Up to 1886, these ships worked alone; from 1886 to 1895, they were employed in connection with ships chartered by the State; actually, *they are immobilized*.

They have repatriated about 12,000 sick or convalescents with only 18 deaths per 1000, notwithstanding the dangers of the voyage across the Indian Ocean and through the Red Sea.

It may be said that these ships were operated hygienically. They have rendered service, not only in repatriation, but also as hospital-ships in Dahomey and Madagascar.

It is particularly interesting to see the service these ships were capable of performing in repatriation. The surgeons fixed the total number to be embarked at 1000 persons, 400 to 500 of whom were sick, half of them bed-ridden. We know this limit was often exceeded, but that was wrong.

In the Marine, the officers, surgeons, and especially the sick, were unanimous in proclaiming the excellence of the system. One of us, after four passages, two of which were return trips, is of the same opinion; the more so because some of these voyages were made under unfavorable conditions, with 1200 and 1300 persons on board.

If a comparison be made between these ships and the chartered vessels, the advantage is not with the latter; while excellent for the transport of well men, they are inferior as transports for the sick.

From 1886 to 1895, the transports of the State have had a mortality of 18 per 1000, while the chartered ships, for the same number of sick, about 12,000, have had a mortality of 26 per 1000.

It is well to remark that, whenever possible, the most serious cases were reserved for the hospital-transports.

The utilization of the chartered ships and the placing in reserve of the transports of the State has thus constituted a *progress backward* from a hygienic standpoint.

Whether the service of repatriation falls upon the State or upon the commercial companies, it is necessary that the ships be fitted up and managed for the special use to which they are to be put.

The fleet of transports to succeed the old ought to be fitted up conformably to the progress of industry and of naval hygiene.

For the ordinary transport service the type *Shamrock* might be suitable, with certain modifications. A ship from 125 to 130 meters in length would be better; it could receive 500 sick with more room for isolation, cleanliness, and disinfection. The lower broadside could have two rows of cots for the less severe cases and for the convalescents; the upper one, a single row for bed-ridden patients. The deck should be reserved for those seriously sick, quartered in special wards, having a special and improved bedding. Isolation and disinfection wards would be necessary.

It would be well to provide steam ventilators for forcing in the fresh and drawing out the foul air.

Distilled water only should be used, for soft water in a hospital, whether ashore or afloat, is a prime necessity. It is necessary then to provide for making it on board in great quantities, and the apparatus must assure a constant supply.

The question of the manufacture of ice aboard ship is not yet practically solved. For some years, the Rouart, an ammonia system, has been tried in the Marine. An apparatus of this type was tried on the *Minerva*, at Gabon; another at Kotonou, during the Dahomey expedition; we understand they did not work very well. A Rouart apparatus was delivered to the *Shamrock*; but when it came to setting it up, great difficulties were encountered; in the first place, a masonry support had to be constructed; then, detailed instructions were lacking. In short, this apparatus, by which cold is obtained by the evaporation of liquefied ammoniacal gas, has never worked; it is not practical for ships.

The *frigorific*, based upon the principle of the expansion of compressed air, and employed upon certain ships of the merchant fleet for the preservation of food, seems to be the most practical apparatus: a motor, which borrows steam from a boiler, forces air into a compressor cylinder, and makes it pass into a detainer.

The illumination should be by electricity.

The funnel should be enveloped by double partitions separated by free spaces, forming a mattress of air.

The water-closets for men and officers ought to be disposed as prescribed by the ministerial despatch of the 13th of February, 1893. A great improvement, carried out upon the hospital-transports of the *Shamrock* type, has been the placing of the closets for the men on the exterior of the ship, permitting the application of the principle, *Everything to the sea*.

The kitchens should be provided with all the utensils necessary for the good working of a hospital.

A cleaning-room and isolation wards are indispensable. Finally, the mechanical windlasses ought to be rendered silent.

CONDITIONS OF REPATRIATION.

When possible, the time of repatriation should be chosen. Attention should be given to the season in which the voyage is to be made, and to the time when the anæmic men, sometimes gravely attacked, will arrive in France. These matters are not indifferent, as is about to be shown.

The percentage of deaths is not the same in the voyages made by the same ships at different periods of the year.

In making an abstract of the deaths which occurred on the 92 voyages from Saigon to France on board the transports of the State and the chartered vessels, during the period from 1886 to 1895, we have the following results:

Leaving Saigon.	Number of Voyages.	Number of Deaths.	Average per Voyage
January	7	37	5.2
February	8	35	4.2
March	6	18	3.0
April	6	30	5.0
May	5	23	4.5
June	6	40	6.6
July	8	68	8.5
August	11	83	7.4
September	10	82	8.2
October	6	26	4.3
November	9	36	4.0
December	10	38	3.8

It is easy to see that the half-year from April to October shows the greater proportion of deaths. The number of voyages was 46, exactly the same as the number during the most favorable half-year, from October to March, which was likewise 46; and nevertheless the difference is more than one-third. During the six months of April, May, June, July, August, and September, we count 326 deaths, giving an average of 6.7 per voyage; during the six other months, we have only 190 deaths, with an average of 4 per voyage.

In the half-year in which most deaths occurred we also remark a notable difference between the first and second quarter. During the months of April, May, and June there were 17 voyages and an average of 5.4 deaths per voyage;

during July, August, and September, there were 29 voyages and 233 deaths, an average of 8.

It is precisely the quarter in which most deaths occurred that shows the greatest number of voyages! This fact is curious, or at least *bizarre*.

The reason might be found in the fact that at this period of the year the number of sick is greater in the colonies and the cases requiring repatriation are more grave. The mortality is, in fact, much greater in Indo-China, in the corresponding periods; were it otherwise, the matter would be incomprehensible.

In studying the figures given by M. Bonnafy, upon the mortality on board the transports and chartered vessels, we find an interesting remark.

From 1879 to 1883, when the sick repatriated from Indo-China all or nearly all came from Saigon, when only six voyages were made a year and the state transports were exclusively used, only a slight difference in the mortality is observed during the passages at different seasons of the year.

Thus for 31 voyages made in five years, with 5399 sick and 95 deaths, or 17.6 per 1000, the following is the record:

Leaving Saigon.	Mortality during the Voyage.
January	12 per 1000
March	16 per 1000
May	16 per 1000
July	18 per 1000
September	17 per 1000
November	22 per 1000

It should be stated that it is difficult to form proper conclusions based upon a relatively small number of sick and a rather limited number of voyages.

The proportions are shown under a different aspect in

considering the voyages made from 1886 to 1895, in the evacuation of all Indo-China.

In 92 passages by the transports of the State and the chartered vessels, with 22,665 sick and 516 deaths, or 18 per 1000 on the transports and 26 per 1000 on the chartered vessels, the following is observed:

Leaving Saigon.	Proportion of Deaths during the Voyage.
January	21 per 1000
February	13 per 1000
March	12 per 1000
April	15 per 1000
May	16 per 1000
June	29 per 1000
July	33 per 1000
August	29 per 1000
September	35 per 1000
October	20 per 1000
November	19 per 1000
December	17 per 1000

The least mortality is observed during February, March, and April; beginning with the month of May, the increase is progressive until October; during November, December, and January, the proportion is a mean between the two extremes.

In short, the most favorable season for repatriation is that of the months February and March; the dangerous period, June, July, August, and September.

The reason is easily seen. In the Indian Ocean the southwest monsoon is very cool; the sea is rough, the air sharp, and diarrhœa reappears. In the Red Sea the heat is overpowering, because there is little breeze and it comes from behind; the heat adds a particular stamp to the diseases, it depresses certain cachectics and deprives them of all resisting power.

In a general way it may be said that the danger of the passage results above all from the gymnastics which should be executed by the skin and the lungs in order to put the body in equilibrium with the surrounding medium. If the temperature jumps up ten degrees and remains there for several days, the cutaneous and pulmonary excretions ought to increase in order to prevent the heat from being concentrated in the organism; this increase of excretions does not take place in the case of men who are too weak. There is an aggravation of the condition of the sick; it is not unusual to observe convalescents overcome by the heat, and a form of delirium which impels cachectics and paludal patients to throw themselves into the sea.

September is the worst month, because it is the hottest in the Red Sea. The higher the sun is, at noon, the higher the temperature; but it is easy to see that the highest temperatures are slightly later than the miximum height of the sun, which is, however, a general rule of Nature, the effect being always posterior to the cause.

The transports of the State were well conceived from the standpoint of hygiene, but were very faulty in regard to speed. Remaining in the neighborhood of the equator is a real hardship for the sick, and the ships of repatriation should have great speed in order to cross the dangerous zone most rapidly.

If the time of crossing the hot seas is not a matter of indifference to the sick, the time of arrival in France has also its importance. Winter is an unfavorable season, and if it is desired to counterbalance the bad effects of the sharp cold of the countries of the North, it is useful to keep the sick for some time in the South. Men who returned from the colonies in a relatively satisfactory condition frequently enter the hospitals a few months later, with a return of diarrhœa or of fever. The sudden changes of temperature are the principal causes of these interminable relapses, which transform men in good enough condition on their arrival into valetudinarians for long months and sometimes for whole years.

Each colony should have at heart the speedy possession of sanitary stations specially reserved for the use of convalescents; there they could await, under very favorable conditions, the propitious time for their return to France.

CHAPTER VI.

Sanitary Police.

All the measures which precede have a real value in increasing the resistance of the men to disease and in assuring them proper care in case they are attacked.

However, certain epidemic diseases, brought from without, as we have shown, develop with such rapidity that it is important, first of all, to prevent access to our possessions; and if this should be impossible, in spite of all vigilance, then to take the most rigorous measures.

§ I. *Commission of Hygiene.*

The organization of a good sanitary police is prescribed in each of our colonies. This should furnish sufficient protection, under the control of the governor, seconded, from a technical standpoint, by the medical authorities.

Formerly the *ordonnateur*, or chief of the health service, represented the surgeons in the council of hygiene; but it is evident that he could not replace them. This anomaly has been suppressed, and with reason, for it is well that each should have the responsibilities of his own functions.

At the present time, in commissions of hygiene, there is place for the president of the council of health, the surgeon of the local service, and the surgeon of the *arraisonements*; but they are not all: the municipal council, the general council, and many other military or civil services are represented there. When it concerns a question of general interest, there is nothing to be said; but in certain cases, when the public health is alone at stake, it is to be feared that a commission so composed might be inspired by considerations foreign to the subject.

Would it not be better to have a permanent commission, which could submit, upon occasion, its opinion, with the reasons therefor, to the governor, charged with making a decision?

We willingly share the views of Doctor Simon relative to the reform of councils of hygiene, and propose to replace them by a commission made up as follows: The chief of the service of health, president; the chief of the service of pharmacy; the chief surgeon of the troops; a civil surgeon; a civil pharmacist; the two latter chosen by the governor.

This purely technical commission, in which the interests of local commerce and of the municipality would find competent defenders, could give a hearing to such persons as it might desire to consult—surgeons, functionaries, or officers—and immediately present its report and conclusions to the governor of the colony.

In case of threatened epidemic, and, above all, of epidemic invasion, there would thus be avoided many idle and sterile discussions, too often ending in the adoption of useless or incomplete measures, or even measures contrary to prudence.

The governor could call for the opinion of the commission of hygiene whenever he considered it necessary to do so, and could convoke that body in case of need.

It is not only indispensable to protect the colonies against the invasion and spread of epidemics, but it must not be forgotten that every contagious disease implanted in one of our possessions becomes a menace to France, on account of the rapidity and frequency of communication.

The prevention of epidemic diseases cannot be accomplished by following an invariable formula. "To combat them with equal energy in all places would be an error of geography; with equal energy at all times, an anachronism."

The system of prevention which ought to be inspired in its details by circumstances and places comprehends: 1. Administrative measures; 2. Hygienic measures.

§ II. *Administrative Measures.*

More authoritative in character than hygienic measures, as M. L. Colin says, the administrative measures would be contrary to the dignity of man, if they alone were employed. Joined with hygienic measures, they are perfectly justified, and may be classed in four groups:

1. The evacuation of epidemic centers.
2. Vaccination.
3. The isolation of contagious diseases.
4. Quarantine.

EVACUATION OF EPIDEMIC CENTERS.

In the presence of certain menacing or declared diseases, the council of hygiene has the right and the duty of preventing assemblies of recent arrivals in the town which is attacked or is under suspicion. The gatherings resulting from the approach of festivals, pilgrimages, etc., should be dissolved, and these solemnities prohibited in case of need. Finally, in the general interest, and aside from extra hygienic prejudice, the council should, above all, order the immediate withdrawal of the troops from the centers of population. It was by withdrawing the soldiers of the white race from Vera Cruz, during the expedition to Mexico, that the frequency of the yellow fever was diminished. In 1884, M. L. Colin did not hesitate to recommend the sending to their homes of all the soldiers of the Army of Paris who were even simply indisposed, to preserve them from the cholera which menaced the garrison.

This would be a measure to take in our possessions in Indo China, whenever there is cause to fear the approach of cholera at the centers. It is, moreover, what is done in case of yellow fever in our colonies of the Antilles.

When the evacuation is ordered, it is an advantage to proceed before the appearance of the plague among the men; otherwise they carry the disease with them and propagate it.

To obviate this dispersion of the plague, it is well, at the time of the evacuation, to isolate the troops by establishing sanitary camps, analogous to those which exist in India, Guadaloupe, and Martinique.

It must be remembered that soldiers can not be camped in the open air, in the colonies, as is done in Europe. It would also be wise, until we shall abandon the towns of the plains for the heights, to erect suitable buildings in these posts of refuge. Now, the huts provided for this use, notwithstanding the services they have rendered, are often in a state of dilapidation which renders their occupancy more dangerous than efficacious, and conditions are sometimes found propitious for bringing to life the germs with which the troops placed there are impregnated.

In Indo-China, in time of cholera, there is a cause of propagation which has not received sufficient attention. This is the possibility of the dissemination of the disease by the natives employed during the day at the European homes in the towns. In the evening, these natives return to their villages, which are often decimated, at certain epochs, by the Asiatic plague. The measures to take, in such a case, seem to us to again depend upon the council of hygiene.

It is the same with measures relative to the agglomerations of natives, principally in the localities inhabited by Europeans.

VACCINATION.

Variola is spread in our colonies to such an extent, and has caused such ravages among the populations subject to our control, that, in their interest as well as in ours, on account of the contagion which is always possible, it has long been a duty to regulate, and even to order, vaccination in our colonial possessions.

Vaccination works very well in Indo-China, especially since the creation of a vaccination center at Saigon, the benefits of which extend over all the Far East.

Vaccination has also been instituted in Senegal and in the Soudan; the Canaques, in New Caledonia, have also been vaccinated.

It is important that administrations as well as populations be impressed with this truth, expressed by L. Colin: Prevention by vaccination is not assured by the performance and success of a single operation; even when successful, it constitutes only the first term of the series of inoculations to impose upon each subject.

In short, revaccinations are indispensable; and if this belief is impressed with difficulty on the minds of the free native populations, we ought never to lose sight of it as far as our native military contingents are concerned.

ISOLATION.

The construction of isolated pavilions for persons attacked by contagious diseases has not always been thought of in the colonial hospitals. It is certain, however, that isolation is an efficacious measure of prevention.

In the absence of special hospitals, there must be an absolute specialization of the wards and pavilions used for those afflicted with contagious diseases—dysenteries, for example.

Without wishing to discuss modes of contagion at this time, we shall confine ourselves to the well-known fact of transmission. A dysenteric placed in the same medium as another patient without signs of intestinal flux can communicate the disease to him.

At least this is what has been reported by Huguet, on board the *Dryade*, in the case of men served with the commodes of their neighbors. It is what was manifestly shown on board the *Loiret*, where the dysenteries coming from Gabon contaminated all the equipage.

More recently, in Senegal, in 1883, in the camp of Kaffa, the Marocains, quartered in straw huts at the rate of ten in each, all contracted dysentery successively as soon as a single one of them carried the germs of the disease into a hut.

Finally, observations more precise and scientific have been made in the hospital of Saint-Mandrier, by Doctor Bertrand, chief surgeon of Marine, who has seen a considerable number of cases contracted in the dysenteric wards.

The military hospital of Noumea, suitable enough in other respects, contains no special wards for dysenteries. It is the same with the military hospital of Saint-Louis in Senegal; it is a large, spacious, two-storied building, but leaves some things to be desired.

The hospital of Saigon is perhaps the best model to give future constructions: It includes a principal pavilion, several other pavilions, and the out-houses. Of late years, pavilions have been constructed which have been well isolated and perfectly adapted for men attacked by contagious diseases. The number and the disposition of the wards permit the complete isolation of dysenteries in special quarters, provided with their own out-buildings.

This system of special pavilions ought to be adopted for all transmissible affections.

With reference to extremely contagious diseases, such as cholera or yellow fever, it would be better to resort to special hospitals removed to a considerable distance. This is the only suitable arrangement; the pavilions annexed to the ordinary hospitals do not accomplish the object, on account of the community of general services.

It would be easy, however, to extemporize, at very small expense, and upon ground reserved for such use, huts which could be burned at the end of the epidemic, with the exception of the metallic frames. Constructions of this kind established in Cochin-China, near Saigon, in 1884, for the isolation of cholera patients, gave excellent results. They should be provided as annexes of the colonial hospitals in all our possessions.

QUARANTINE.

The quarantine of ships, the temporary sequestration of their passengers, the disinfection, and, if necessary, sanitary unloading, until recently constituted all the means for closing a port of our colonies to certain plagues.

The decree of these measures pertains to the council of hygiene, and it is chiefly in regard to yellow fever and cholera that vigilance and severity should be doubled.

To-day the tendency of the French sanitary police is to substitute for the preventive measures taken on arrival, measures taken at the point of departure and during the voyage. This tendency has been aproved by all the international sanitary conferences of recent years, and has resulted in a complete change from former requirements.

Ships coming from contaminated countries, if they have been regularly disinfected at the point of departure or during the voyage and if the sanitary conditions on board are satisfactory, can obtain *pratique* on arrival, even with an unclean bill of health. Such is the base of the new regulation of maritime sanitary police.

Thus, in France, the quarantine of observation, which was the rule for ships coming from countries suspected of cholera or yellow fever, has been replaced by a medical inspection upon arrival, but *a thorough and rigid inspection*.

This change constitutes in itself an immense advance and a great advantage to commerce, which has shown its appreciation by improving the hygienic condition of its ships.

A decree, of date the 31st of March, 1897, publishes the regulations of the maritime sanitary police in the colonies and countries of the protectorate of the French Republic. This new measure is absolutely justified.

Indeed, as MM. Brouardel and Proust have judiciously remarked, disinfection is the first means to employ to prevent the importation of morbific germs. Prolong the quarantine for weeks, and, once terminated, allow the passengers to leave with their baggage full of infected linen or their clothing contaminated, and you have prevented nothing— you have only prescribed a vexatious measure to trouble commercial interests, and you have in no way guarded the public health.

Disinfection, on the contrary, makes quarantine useless and gives a complete guaranty from a sanitary point of view. If it is properly performed at the point of departure or during a long voyage, a medical inspection at the port of arrival will suffice. If the measures have been well taken and the testimony of the surgeon is worthy of credence, *pratique* may be safely accorded.

The corollary of these benevolent and liberal measures would be the installation, in the lazarets of our colonies, of apparatus for disinfection by vapor under pressure, like those of the ports of France. These apparatus should also be found on all the troop-transports.

With disinfection on departure and during the voyage, the use of lazarets will become less and less necessary, and they may be advantageously replaced by simple sanitary stations a short distance from the ports. These stations would be of more service than the lazarets; they could receive the sick, if provided with disinfection *matériel*.

Finally, in the colonies, where eruptive fevers, chiefly variola, and also diphtheria, are feared almost as much as cholera, great watchfulness is necessary. If a ship arrive with sick attacked by eruptive fevers, disinfection should be proceeded with before permission is given to hold communication with the shore. The same is true of typhus, with regard to which too great precautions cannot be taken.

These remarks are the more important, as the last affections have not been provided for by the maritime sanitary regulations of the parent State. Indeed, in France, these affections being considered as indigenous, less care has been taken regarding their importation by the maritime route.

§ III. *Hygienic Measures.*

It remains for us to consider the truly hygienic measures, which are of two kinds: disinfection and the sanitation of towns.

DISINFECTION.

The first thing to be done in case of an epidemic is to disseminate the troops before the plague attacks them; but before this a system of disinfection should have been provided. The interests of the population, as well as of the soldiers, demand prompt and effective action on the part of the authorities. The epidemic germ must be suppressed, as far as possible, from the moment it appears.

Cholera and yellow fever, of which we have cited only too many examples, have reappeared after an interval of years, solely because contaminated clothing was not destroyed and apparel and bedding, used by the sick, were not disinfected or were disinfected imperfectly.

Disinfection should not be left to the initiative of commanding officers, nor to that of the civil authorities, European or native. Its importance is great and its execution should be surrounded by all the guaranties for the common safety. Upon the recommendation of the council of hygiene, the chief of the colony himself should order it, and the civil and military powers should act in concert and give mutual aid in the performance of the work on which the safety of all depends.

Every large colonial town should be provided with several apparatus:

1. Geneste-Herscher stoves would suffice for the sanitary work of both the garrison and the population.

2. The Vaillard transportable stove would answer for secondary posts.

3. The small centers or isolated posts should receive steeping-vats, with sufficient instructions for their use when required.

There should likewise be a supply of sulphur, bichloride of mercury, sulphate of copper, chloride of lime, and chloride of zinc, at the disposition of the council of hygiene of each colonial town, or of its representative, who would naturally be the surgeon, in the least important centers. These are necessary for protection, by all the measures of disinfection ordered, either in view of a possible epidemic, or after ascertaining that a case exists at any point, whether simply suspected or positively known to be of a contagious nature.

When he considers it expedient, the surgeon delegated by the sanitary council should centralize the service of disinfection in order to take charge of its direction, and should come to an understanding with the senior surgeon on duty with the troops of the garrison, to the end that identical measures may be taken in the barracks.

In case of epidemic localized in barracks, the military authority should take the initiative, but not without informing the council of hygiene. In a word, there should always be complete harmony upon this point between all the powers, and unity of views and of action, the enemy being the same for everybody.

The case must also be provided for when posts without surgeons, or isolated columns, may have to resort to disinfection, and that upon their own initiative, in the event of epidemic danger, or of a contagious or suspected case, or upon the receipt of orders emanating from the council of hygiene and transmitted direct. It is also necessary that the post commander should possess a short, detailed, and very clear manual of instructions, indicating the manner of using the apparatus and substances at his disposition. The following is an outline of such instructions:

Disinfection of Premises.—A solution of 50:1000 of sulphate of copper (blue copperas) is an excellent disinfectant for sinks, water-conduits, and water-closets. The same may be said of a solution of chloride of zinc. In default of these substances, chloride of lime, commonly called chlorine, employed under the form of a thick milk, is very good, but inferior to the preceding on account of its odor and its inferiority as a germicide. If sulphur is available (either the flowers of sulphur or, better still, roll-sulphur), it may be very suitably used for disinfection, not in open places, but in bed-rooms, dormitories of the men, or wards of a hospital. It may be said, however, that this operation is not always easy in the colonies on account of the numerous openings, and the fact is regrettable, because the vapor of the sulphur permits the attainment, at a single blow, of the sanitation of places and the disinfection of clothing and bedding, which can be spread out or otherwise suitably disposed. The mattresses can also be disinfected in this manner, at least on the surface, for they are too thick to be completely penetrated by the sulphurous vapor.

After having found the cubical contents of the room, closed the openings and seams, opened the furniture, spread out the hangings and all the objects to be disinfected, the sulphur, at the rate of 40 grams per cubic meter, is placed on common plates and sprinkled with a little alcohol; it is then set on fire, and one retires through a door left free. This is immediately closed and all the joints stopped up on the outside, in case the sulphurous vapor is seen to filter through. A good precaution to take at the outset consists in sprinkling the floor and walls of the room to be disinfected, which favors the development and action of the sulphurous acid. The room remains closed at least twenty-four hours; it is then opened, washed, dried, and all the objects it contains are aired.

Another excellent means of disinfecting contaminated rooms is to wash the floors and walls with a large sponge saturated with an alcoholic solution of bichloride of mercury of 1:1600. After this washing, they are allowed to dry, and are then repainted and whitewashed. This disinfection ought to be carried into all the angles and crevices, without leaving a nook not penetrated by the liquid. It should precede all sweeping and cleaning. For painted surfaces it might be followed by a washing with potash, and even by scraping.

The atomizers long used for this purpose had perhaps the advantage of spreading the liquids more uniformly; but it has been observed that they do not cause a sufficient penetration of the surfaces, at least unless they are allowed to play for a long time on the same spot.

Those who are charged with these operations should

remember that they are handling deadly poisons and should be careful not to carry their hands to the mouth; when all is finished, they ought to wash very carefully in warm water and with soap.

Disinfection of Clothing.—In the large centers, the Geneste-Herscher or Vaillard apparatus or steeping-vats may be used. The important thing is to submit the objects to the action of vapor under pressure, at 110 to 120 degrees. In the small places, a suitable apparatus can be constructed at very little expense, in a manner described by Doctor Richard, a chief surgeon in the Army. A boiler or a pot is taken and covered very exactly with a cask without heads, the upper orifice only being provided with a cover pierced with two holes, one receiving a thermometer and the other permitting the escape of the vapor. A fire is lighted under the boiler; when the thermometer marks 100 degrees, one waits an hour, and then removes the clothes, hung upon rods for disinfection. The temperature rises to 103 and 105 degrees in the thickness of the textures placed in the vapor bath; this results in a satisfactory purification.

Attention is also called to even a more simple method of disinfecting linen. This disinfection must be made, be it understood, before washing, else it would be useless; indeed, those called upon to wash it would be exposed to the greatest danger, as has often been proved. The linen is thrown into pails filled with a solution of bichloride of mercury of 2:1000. It is allowed to remain there twenty-four hours, and is then put in boiling water to remove the bichloride of mercury.

The bichloride solution is harmless to clothing, hangings, and objects of equipment; this is not the case, however, with boiling water. Objects susceptible to injury should not, then, be boiled, but only the linen. Moreover, the objects which would be injured by boiling are generally much less contaminated. It will suffice to leave them for an hour or two in the solution and then rinse them with soft, cold water.

The wool of mattresses is likewise susceptible to injury; it should be disinfected in an ordinary or improvised stove by the use of steam.

All persons who have approached the sick, whether accidentally or in a continuous manner, should disinfect their clothing before resuming ordinary life.

The question often arises as to what objects it is possible to disinfect and what it is prudent to destroy. After a slight epidemic of cholera on board, one of us proceeded in a manner which may serve as a guide. All that had been in immediate contact with the patient and was manifestly contaminated by ejections or sweat was destroyed; all that was not so polluted was disinfected. By acting thus, we believe unnecessary destruction can be avoided without sacrificing the rigorous conditions of hygienic requirements.

Disinfection of Objects and Utensils Used by the Sick.—The glasses, plates, cups, canteens, forks, and all articles which have served the sick, should be washed in a solution of sulphate of copper and then placed in boiling water.

Disinfection of Ejections.—The alvine discharges and the vomitings should be collected in porcelain receptacles at the bottom of which is left a disinfecting solution; enough solution will be added to cover them completely. They should never be thrown into the latrines, nor into rivers, but into holes dug for the purpose. There they should be immediately covered with lime, charcoal, and earth.

Disinfection of Cadavers.—In case of death, the cadaver should be rapidly and thoroughly washed with a bichloride solution, and then enveloped in a shroud saturated with the same solution. The sawdust from the bier, with charcoal added, should likewise be thoroughly saturated with the same solution.

Prophylactic Disinfection of Personnel and Matériel.—Those who are called upon to attend the sick should be chosen from among the most courageous and most intelligent. If it is a question of typhoid fever or of variola, men will be chosen in preference who have had these diseases.

The hygienic instructions ought to be explained and rigorously carried out. As for those who are necessarily brought into contact with the patient, they should be extremely careful in regard to cleanliness, above all avoiding carrying the hands to the mouth; they should wash often, with the bichloride solution or with sulphate of copper, not only the hands, but also the face. Soldiers employed on this service should have no communication with their comrades, still less with those outside. They should receive special food and supplementary rations.

The clothing of the attendants should receive the same disinfection as that worn by the patients.

The litters, vehicles, and boats should be disinfected in accordance with their character; for that purpose a special atomizer may be used with advantage.

SANITATION OF LOCALITIES.

The sanitation of localities—and, we would willingly add, of populations—is a necessary precaution. It will serve to render the invasion and extension of diseases, whatever their nature, less frequent and less formidable.

It is known in Europe, especially in England, that a contagious disease has less chance of gaining a foothold, when the country is refractory, or is, as is said in England with reference to cholera, *cholera-proof*.

The most hygienic towns are those which have an irreproachable potable water, a system of drainage and cleaning to prevent the soil from being polluted; those where sewers are kept in good order and the lodgings and sales of drinks supervised; where vaccination is prescribed and the examination of public women is regularly made; those, in short, which have abattoirs well managed and well located, suitable hospitals, sufficient means of disinfection, and special vehicles for those who are sick with contagious diseases. In such towns, hygienically constructed and hygienically governed, the mortality diminishes year by year.

In the colonies, where institutions and customs of this kind are more necessary than elsewhere, everyone knows what really exists and divines what ought to be done. With the exception of Saigon and a few new centers in Tong-King, most of our colonial towns are regular sewers, where care for hygiene is a thing unknown. The local administration is not stimulated by the fear of seeing the garrisons suppressed, and it often opposes a great force of inertia to the just demands of military authority.

The council of hygiene is never consulted except upon the approach of an epidemic, although all questions concerning the health of the troops and inhabitants should be regularly submitted to it. Every vexatious thing that happens in the colonies is charged to the soldier, and the question of what diseases are given him is never raised. If the towns of the littoral were to be evacuated and the troops placed in the health cities, upon the heights, many of these inconveniencies would be avoided. The municipalities themselves would understand what they have to do in the way of quartering the troops, and what would be necessary to keep the ones remaining with them. The conditions of living and of general health would be more satisfactory for all, and the measures of edileship and of urban hygiene would benefit the whole population.

CHAPTER VII.

Special Measures for Expeditions.

When an expedition is undertaken in a country beyond the seas, it is necessary to be informed of all the difficulties to be overcome. In considering the climatic and telluric dangers, a general formula will not suffice; even in the same latitudes, the hot countries are subject to various conditions and influences, and the means of preservation are different.

San Domingo and Mexico awaken thoughts of yellow fever, and the European about to be exposed there would be guilty if he did not remember, from the very first, to provide against its attack.

In Cochin-China and Tong-King are found the germs of dysentery, diarrhea, and cholera; measures should therefore be taken, at the time of an expedition, to avoid these intestinal diseases.

Senegal, Dahomey, and Madagascar are the homes of paludism, and it is principally against malaria that protection is needed.

The judicious application of scientific information upon the distribution of diseases in the world is capable, in itself alone, of averting great disasters. The French expedition to San Domingo, at the beginning of this century, might have had a different ending from that which history records, if the conditions of the genesis and propagation of yellow fever had been better known. Our expedition to Mexico, so murderous in the beginning, would have been much more so if it had not been remembered that yellow fever never quits the littoral to advance into the interior. What would have happened without the Convention of Soledad, which permitted the army to leave the hot lands for a less dangerous zone?

Every expedition in the hot countries, whether it be within the limits of one of our possessions or upon foreign shores, should be wisely and prudently studied before being decided upon and undertaken.

§ I. *Colonial Expeditions.*

There are two kinds of colonial expeditions: the first are local in nature, constituting a condition of campaign for the whole or a part of the local garrison, whether it concerns the suppression of a rebellion or the extension of our influence over the neighboring countries; the others are those great expeditions decreed by the Government with a view to operating in the Tropics, or in a region in order to conquer it.

In the first case, all ought to be arranged in advance; the colony in mobilizing its military forces, should have a well-determined plan providing for all necessities.

In the case of a distant expedition, a colonial expedition proper, the first care, after the operation is decided upon, is to choose the chief and to judiciously constitute the head of that complex organism, an expeditionary corps.

In the first place, the chief of the expedition ought to be chosen, without regard to any irrelevant prejudice, from among those best qualified by reason of their antecedents and individual service.

To this chief should be added three assistants: a chief of staff, an officer of the administrative service or commissary, and a surgeon.

Upon this body, constituted as a superior staff, is to fall, thenceforth, the preparation of all the details of the expedition, each member being more especially charged with the questions relative to his own department.

It is indispensable for this staff to have a sufficient knowledge of the country where the operations are to take place; otherwise, it would be impossible to make proper arrangements for quartering, camping, subsisting, clothing, and equipping the troops, and would be difficult to prepare for supplies and transports.

In order to attend to the smallest details of organization, to receive the troops upon their arrival from Europe, and to superintend the arrangements preliminary to active operations, the commander-in-chief should be one of the first to arrive at the base of operations.

The English, whose practical genius we cannot help admiring when it is a question of organizing a colonial expedition, have taught us valuable lessons. After many reverses sustained at the end of the last and the beginning of the present century, due to a disdain of hygiene and climatology, our neighbors have profited by the lessons of experience; it is known how they have succeeded.

It is well to be inspired with the general spirit which characterized one of their most fortunate expeditions, both from a military and sanitary point of view.

The commander-in-chief arrived at the base of operations more than a month before the expeditionary corps, accompanied by a technical *personnel*, including a large number of surgeons. He made sure of the application of all the necessary measures to preserve the troops from variola and yellow fever. He also had a ship fitted up to serve as a floating hospital and prescribed a system to be followed in removing the sick.

The troops were to arrive in the good season, with a uniform appropriate to the torrid climate; a short and roomy tunic of flannel or of gray serge, with long side pockets; trousers of the same material, closed to the leg by leggings of brown holland; and a light helmet. Each man carried, in addition, two shirts, a flannel band, a waterproof, a small pocket filter, and an air filter, intended to be placed before the mouth to prevent the absorption of miasma.

Moreover, each soldier was in possession of a clearly worded hygienic manual relating to the personal hygiene of the soldier. Numerous bearers had been enrolled for the service of the columns, and the route to be followed was marked by halting-places 20 kilometers apart. At each of these places was found a camp capable of sheltering a thousand men and composed of large huts with circular campbeds, upon which 50 sleepers could stretch themselves out comfortably. Each of these halting-places included also a special hut for the officers, store-houses, a field hospital, kitchens, a water supply, and a large filter.

This campaign, so skillfully prepared, was that of Ashantee. It is a custom to cite it as a model, but it is not alone. Begun in January, 1874, it was finished in March, and on the 23d of that month the European regiments again took the route to England.

General Wolseley had operated rapidly and with a sacrifice of only 65 lives out of a force of 4000 men, of whom 2000 were Europeans.

Later, and not far from the same place, the administration of the French Marine was largely inspired by these principles. General Dodds attempted all, but with less perfect means of putting them in practice. He was also at a disadvantage in having younger troops. Our two campaigns in Dahomey were likewise well conducted, especially the second, considering the desperate resistance of the enemy and the difficulties of every nature to be overcome.

The campaign of 1895 in Madagascar was disastrous, because it was wished to make innovations by attempting a trial of continental war in the great Malagasy Island! Now, the success of colonial expeditions will long be subordinated, not so much to skillful dispositions of the most subtle strategy, as to a harmony of absolutely special natural conditions and to the observance of hygienic measures.

In their last campaign on the coast of Africa, from the 14th of December, 1895, to the 3d of February, 1896, the English also obtained surprising results. From the report of the surgeon, Colonel W. Taylor, there were only 7 deaths out of 999 Europeans present. Adding 3 deaths which occurred on the return voyage, there results a total of 10 deaths out of 999 European officers and soldiers, or 1 per cent. Out of 375 natives, there was only a single death, giving 0.25 per cent.

It is true that this campaign was very short and not at all murderous, which must be taken into account in the comparisons. However, it is impossible to deny the excellence of the result.

§ II. *Choice of Troops.*

In the first place, the commander-in-chief should determine the strength and nature of the effective force to set in motion. It is only upon this information, well established, that the accessory services will be able to make their arrangements and fix the limits of their coöperation.

To avoid the risk of sending too small a force, it is not necessary to err in the opposite direction. Those who had experience of the country asked themselves, with reason, before the Madagascar expedition, if it were really necessary to mobilize 15,000 men to fight the Hovas, especially as the difficulties of supply seemed very great. With 4000 well-chosen Europeans and 8000 natives the work would have been easy.

The effective force to be employed having once been

determined, it is necessary to designate the units which are to make up the expeditionary corps. Experience shows that these should be taken from the corps which ordinarily go to the colonies, and accessorily from the Algerian corps. The metropolitan army is not intended for campaigns beyond the seas; the soldiers are accustomed to the garrisons of France and are not at all prepared for colonial expeditions; special men are needed for this purpose, and this fact cannot be too strongly emphasized.

Choice should then be made, among the men of these special corps, of those who are exempt from the least defect, and also from those who are accustomed to colonial life; provided there be among the latter neither old paludal patients, candidates for a yellow fever attack, nor former dysenteries, predisposed to diarrhœa and congestion of the liver, nor those subject to bronchial affections, probable consumptives, nor those troubled with rheumatism. The medical examination should be most severe and conducted by a technical commission, and not by a single surgeon.

Men who are too young ought not to be used in wars in the Tropics; we have seen the enormous mortality of soldiers from 19 to 23 years of age. In all our expeditions, and in the English expeditions too, the same fact has been observed. If in Dahomey, in 1892, the Foreign Legion had only 35 per 1000 invalidations, while the *infanterie de marine* had 90, the flotilla 80, the artillery 74, the engineers 50, etc., it was because the soldiers of the Legion are older and in consequence more robust. Moreover, they are men inured to all fatigue, little accessible to moral depression, and apt in making the best of the most precarious resources. The majority of the soldiers of the Marine, on the contrary, are men from 19 to 23 years old who have never served in the colonies, are depressed at the first attacks of paludism, and are more accessible to discouragement. Excellent soldiers, full of courage and ardor, they lack bottom, because they are too young, because their constitutions are not fully developed, and—we will add with one of their generals, who will pardon us for expressing his opinion, which is our own in all points —because their military instruction has often been too forward.

The campaign of Madagascar has proved the same thing with regard to troops of different arms and varied composition. It likewise permitted the verification of a fact brought to light in preceding campaigns: that it is necessary, to the greatest possible extent, to prefer native troops to white troops, since the former pay a tribute to torrid climates three or four times less costly than our own.

Thus the Algerian tirailleurs disembarked 1600 men at Majunga. One battalion of this force was with General Metzinger from the beginning. They brought 900 before Tananarivo; the men of the Legion were equally fortunate.

The 200th of the Line, composed of volunteers from 20 to 22 years old, and for the most part less than a year with the colors, had an effective strength of 2700 men, of whom 300 were recruits; it was possible to preserve until the end of the operations only 163. The 40th Battalion of Chasseurs, formed under the same conditions, did not arrive before the capital of the island at all, and out of 700 men, only 120 returned to France.*

There is one consideration, however, which should not be lost sight of in organizing an expedition: it is the necessity of not removing native soldiers entirely from their own country. The idea of making the Annamites serve in the Soudan, or the Senegalese in Indo-China or Guiana, if it were ever

---

*In Bénin, in 1890, the white troops lost 46 per 1000; the natives, only 19.

put in practice, would give results only infinitely worse than those produced by the use of white troops in the same countries.

Recall in this connection the susceptibility of the blacks to cholera, the complete unfamiliarity of the Indo-Chinese races with yellow fever, etc., not to speak of the discouragement which would take possession of natives transplanted in a climate totally strange to them.

The creoles, like the blacks, could render us excellent service at their homes. This is a point which should not be disdained, especially at the time of an expedition.

Since the law of the 1st of August, 1895, relating to military service, Reunion can furnish every year a contingent of about 800 men. That is the worth of a battalion, and of a regiment for the three contingents of the active army. The Marine has it in hand to take 2400 men ready to be levied in Madagascar.

The battalion of volunteers of Reunion was recruited under the worst possible conditions, and nevertheless has shown good powers of resistance: Out of an effective strength of 549 men, officers and Europeans not included, the proportion of sick or convalescents withdrawn was 28.4 per cent, and the proportion of deaths did not exceed 3.09 per cent.

This recent example augurs well for the services of the young creoles of Reunion, once they are well instructed and organized.

Doctor Théron has remarked that the nearer the conscript approached the white race in color—and with stronger reason the white creole—the more cause there was for his exemption from service; the more traces of African blood there were in the conscript, the better were his chances of being declared physically good. From this it would appear that the effectives furnished by Reunion should include a very small proportion of white creoles, and that the colored creoles should be in great majority, calling by this name both the creoles of the centers and also those with little trace of white blood from the heights.

The European element is an indispensable factor in the organization of the natives. It sustains the creole troops and furnishes on the battle-field that *old guard* which decides the victory. This reserve, few in numbers, ought to be of proved solidity, a veritable phalanx, seasoned to disease as well as to bullets; it ought to be composed of the *élite*, chosen from the best colonial corps, and in order to form it the authorities should not recoil from any sacrifice.

§ III. *Convoys and Supplies.*

The question of convoys and supplies, which enters into the preparation of every well-planned expedition, has always received great attention from the chiefs of expedition, especially in the hot countries. It is not an easy thing to provide food and munitions for a column advancing into a country, sometimes unknown, and where there are neither roads nor paths; it is still more difficult to provide for the transport of the sick, who must be taken to the rear.

It is, first of all, necessary that the *matériel* sent from France arrive at the base of operations at the proper time, that it be placed in the shelter of suitable store-houses, and that it be forwarded to the troops on the march and to the detached posts all along the line of operations.

To perform these numerous duties, it is necessary to have transport animals and a number of native coolies proportionate to the effective combatant strength, taking into account the necessity which will often exist of having the packs of the soldiers carried by the auxiliaries.

If the supplies can be forwarded by water-ways, in place

of enrolling only the bearers, it will be necessary to look out for boats, pirogues, and oarsmen in sufficient number, according to the quantity of stores to be transported and the length of the route.

The principle is to never transform the soldier, especially the European combatant, into a coolie. A heavy load should not be imposed upon the white troops in the Tropics, and all the skill of the general should be directed towards disposing a convoy in such a way that no fatigue for the combatants will result from carrying an excessive weight.

The Bearers.—It is necessary to have a sufficient number of bearers: that is the difficulty of every colonial expedition, and it was on account of deficiency in this respect, during the Madagascar campaign, that use was made of troops for the unloading of *matériel*, the construction of roads, and the transport of food.

Besides, it is sufficient to see the care taken by the chiefs of expedition to collect armies of bearers to follow their columns of operation. They are necessary impedimenta; without bearers, a colonial expedition is impossible.

During the expedition to China, in 1860, the English army of 10,000 men had a convoy of 2500 animals, in charge of 200 conductors, assisted by 300 coolies, while our 3000 French troops had only 1000 bearers to transport all their *matériel*. A little later, in Cochin-China, we were able to organize a corps of 1800 natives charged with the convoys.

In Abyssinia, in 1867, the English had more than 9000 auxiliaries of this kind, commanded by Europeans.

For their convoys on the expedition against the Ashantees, our neighbors made use not only of men, but also of the women of the West Coast, long accustomed to this trade, which they carried on for the merchants of the littoral. Nevertheless, the English one day found themselves in a delicate situation on account of a momentary defection among their auxiliaries, and no one knows what would have happened but for the energetic and intelligent initiative of the corps commander: General Wolseley immediately called into requisition the native soldiers of the West India Regiment, and for fifteen days confided to them the functions abandoned by the negro deserters. The expedition suffered no delay, but only cost a little more, for the general rightly believed it to be his duty under such circumstances to pay liberally for the special services of the native soldiers.

In Egypt, in 1885, the English collected 7000 Soudanese as bearers; and they placed under the orders of a major, to fill that office during the campaign in Zululand, 2000 natives, levied upon the frontiers of Natal.

The Russians in their campaigns in Central Asia have likewise had recourse to immense convoys. In 1880, Skobeleff had no less than 21,000 camels at his disposition.

Let us now see what we have done of late years:

In Upper Senegal, the first column of 1880, for an effective force of 500 combatants, had no less than 500 native bearers.

In Tong-King, the organization of the corps of coolies during the expedition was the constant care of our generals, and yet our men were very often much more burdened than was suitable.

General Bouët collected 500 bearers before the march upon Sontay; General Millot, more than 6000, of whom 2000 accompanied the first brigade advancing towards Bac-Ninh. Each group of 50 bearers was commanded by a *caï* (Annamite corporal).

Before advancing upon Lang-Son, General Brière de l'Isle likewise paid special attention to the organization of a large convoy.

Useful Precautions.—If the authorities ought first of all

to demand of the coolies sufficient strength to carry a load of 20 to 25 kilograms, the maximum to impose on a black, the hygienist, on his part, has the duty of watching over the health of the auxiliaries. They ought to be healthy and exempt from all contagious disease.

If they have not been vaccinated, they should be required to submit to the preventive inoculation, in view of the frequency of variola in certain countries.

The *personnel* of the convoy is the mainspring of the expedition; let an epidemic attack it, and the combatants in their turn will soon be struck.

If the coolies fail, what would be done regarding supplies and the transportation of the sick and wounded? The general will not always be able, like the English on the African coast, to utilize black troops for that purpose, and in default of bearers, the expedition might be gravely compromised. To care for the convoy and watch over the well-being of those connected with it is then a necessity for the chief who wishes to be successful. *The hygiene of the bearer is the health of the soldier.*

As for the manner in which the coolies carry their load, it is of no importance; whether upon the head or upon the shoulders, all depends on the country and the customs of the natives.

To spare the bearers, it is well to have a large number of animals. In the expedition of Chitral, in the north of India, the English had 11,600 camels and 26,000 mules. In our possessions there are pack-mules which ought to give the best results, unless it is possible to use water-ways.

The Convoys in Madagascar.—By the avowal of the Government itself, the cause of all our troubles in Madagascar was the lack of bearers. Even at a late hour, there were only 7000 coolies and 6000 mules.

Enrollment should have been made at the outset of 10,000 Kabyles, 5000 Senegalese, and 5000 Sakalaves, and they should have been brigaded before the arrival of the troops. It was one preliminary operation of the highest importance, and of which the examples of the English in Abyssinia and at the Gold Coast, and of General Dodds in Dahomey, should have made us think.

We are of the opinion that the idea of using vehicles was truly unfortunate. To pull a vehicle a quadruped is necessary, and in order that it may travel there must be a road, without counting the drivers.

It has been calculated that a mule pulls 200 kilograms in a vehicle and can carry only 100, from which must be deducted the food of itself and its conductor, or 10 kilograms. Now, 6000 pack-mules and 20,000 coolies, collected in advance, would have been able to transport the same load as 6000 mules in harness; they would have permitted an advance to be made without waiting for reinforcements of animals and drivers, which could then have been sent from France or elsewhere in proportion to the needs. The deadly stoppage of the troops at Suberbieville would have been considerably shortened, and the road intended for the circulation of the vehicles would have been unnecessary.

Moreover, if the advice of Admiral Bienaimé had been taken, all the operations of transport and supplies could have taken place by the river; the expedition would have been more prompt, more decisive, and much less murderous.

This is truly the place to destroy a legend, false like most legends, about the *rôle* of the Marine at Madagascar. Maurice Loir has perfectly demonstrated that this *rôle* was quite other than has been depicted.

The commandant of the naval division of the Indian Ocean explained the measures to be taken, from the commencement of 1895, in case the road to Tananarivo, by way of Majunga, should be adopted.

This route, which was preferred by Colonel de Beylié, was longer than that from Tamatave, but was infinitely better adapted to the march of an important column, and had, besides, a precious advantage: that of permitting the utilization, for a good part of the way, of the great river Betsiboka, which, emptying into the sea before Majunga, is navigable for ships of light draught.

In his report of the 30th of May, 1894, the commandant of the division asked for the naval *matériel* appropriate to this navigation: 50 lighters, 12 tugs, and several gun-boats. Alluding even to the military question, he recommended that the troops be sent in two installments: the first, of 2500 men (robust and seasoned, formed from the Foreign Legion and the *infanterie de marine*) to arrive in March-April; the second, the main body, to arrive about the 15th of May—that is to say, at the height of the dry season, a favorable time for the expedition. So regulated, the troops of the advance guard would have occupied, from April, the two banks of the river, in a location near the sea; they would have driven off the enemy, thus assuring free navigation to the gun-boats and tugs. The main body, ascending the river with the flotilla, would have rapidly crossed the low regions of the island—that is to say, the hot lands and the marshes. It was the means of most surely avoiding, without too much loss, the fever, the most precious ally of the Hovas.

In order to properly carry out this programme it was necessary to know thoroughly the character of the Betsiboka. Some time before the expedition, Midshipman Compagnon, of the *Primauguet*, passing himself off as an agent of the mining company of Suberbie, was sent upon a steamer of that company, and took bearings and soundings.

In the interval, aided by some companies of *infanterie de marine* from Diego-Suarez and Reunion, Admiral Bienaimé was successful in a military occupation of Tamatave, the 11th of December, 1894, and of Majunga, the 16th of January, 1895. These two operations were accomplished without noise and without serious resistance, which led the commander-in-chief to say in his letter to the Minister, and with an accurate perception of the future: "It is known that no serious resistance is to be feared and that all efforts should be directed to the organization of the service and the movement of the convoys."

Majunga once chosen as the place of disembarkment, an apparatus was installed upon the shore for distilling sea water, as soft water is rare upon the margins of that vast bay. Then the entrance channel was marked with buoys to warn all ships coming there for the first time of the difficulties of making land; finally, the Malagasies were recruited to serve as bearers or navvies—that is to say, as auxiliaries of the Army at the time of its taking the field.

Admiral Bienaimé had been careful to inform the Minister that the recruitment of the Malagasies would be very difficult and insufficient. In default of Chinese, always cholera suspects, he would have to resort to the blacks of the African coast.

The lack of coolies imposed a great excess of burdens on the Marine; but, under the impulsion of its chief, it was able to accomplish prodigies in the unloading of the ships and transports in the river. With the aid of a company of *infanterie de marine*, Maroway was seized on the 2d of May, 1895, a new proof that the operations could have been conducted by the river.

§ IV. *Sanitary Service.*

A sanitary organization prepared for a continental war

cannot be used in a colonial campaign without modification. In this connection, the Madagascar campaign is instructive.

The theory of the field hospital is based on European war: it advances at the same time as the troops and a distance determined beforehand; it can be installed in villages and houses requisitioned; quarters and beds are found there and also indispensable accessories, such as kitchens and laundries; to begin operations, it is only necessary to open the bottle-cases and paniers.

These dispositions are not applicable in the colonies, where nothing is provided, as a rule. It is therefore necessary to take up all the questions relative to the organization of the health service: *personnel*, *matériel*, transport of the sick, location of the hospitals, and evacuation.

PERSONNEL.

The chief of the health service of the expeditionary corps should be of high rank, should have local experience, and should possess the absolute confidence of the commander-in-chief of the expedition.

The surgeons should be chosen among those who have a knowledge of the country and experience in colonial expeditions. They should be in great number.

The regiments should have their complete medical effective: 6 surgeons to the regiment, 2 to the battalion, and this number should be increased by 2 as substitutes, making a total of 8.

The sanitary organizations should likewise have their complete effective, increased one-third to fill unforeseen vacancies caused by the establishment of posts along the line of supplies.

We have always been too parsimonious. In Dahomey, in 1892, the sanitary *personnel* was too small. For 1432 European and 2176 native combatants, we had only 18 surgeons: 9 with the column, 5 in the hospitals of Porto-Novo and Kotonou, 4 on the *Mytho* and the convoy ships. This number was too small; with the column, and in the hospitals especially, it should have been doubled. The deficiency would have been more noticeable if the expedition had not been so successful.

In Madagascar, in 1895, the number of surgeons was much too small. The troops were provided with 2 surgeons to a battalion, or 24 for the European regiments. The sanitary organizations were supplied with a variable number of surgeons and pharmacists, according to their importance. The sanitarium was sufficiently supplied, but the hospital of evacuation and the field hospitals were lacking in *personnel*.

If we had adopted the proportion of surgeons sent to the Gold Coast by the English in 1873, there would have been more than 300 sent to Madagascar. It was thought sufficient to send 80 for the 15,000 to 16,000 combatants, to which number must be added 7000 auxiliaries. The proportion was almost identical with that in Dahomey; it was very insufficient.

The pharmacists are useful in the sanitary organizations and should not be forgotten.

There should be a sufficient number of veterinarians to give the necessary care to the animals of the convoy; 20 were sent to Madagascar and they were efficient in caring for the 6000 mules. It was anxiously asked if the mules could live in Madagascar; they did very well, because they were admirably cared for.

The nurses should be numerous, also. In Dahomey, outside of the regimental nurses and auxiliaries, there were only 20 Europeans and 6 natives. In Madagascar a greater number had been provided; 1 nurse had been sent for 5 hospital beds, and as the number of beds for the various organizations was 3000, the total number of nurses was 600.

Nevertheless they were insufficient, since nurses fall sick as well as soldiers. Three months after the arrival, it was not rare to find a sanitary organization practically unprovided with nurses. In August, at the hospital of Ankaboka, there were only 4 well nurses for 1000 sick; at Suberbieville, there were only 6 nurses for 600 sick.

It must also be said that in the French Army we have no regular corps of nurses, as in the German, where special corps of them exist. Our nurses are scarcely initiated in hospital life before they return home. The colonial army, when it is formed, should possess professional nurses, like the Marine. This is not only necessary, it is indispensable.

MATÉRIEL.

In a colonial expedition, such an incumbrance as the complicated equipage which follows an army corps in Europe is not to be thought of: surgical and administrative wagons, wagons of supply and reserve, tents and barracks.

It is necessary, however, to transport dressing materials, medicines, food for the sick, and shelters or the materials to construct them; it will also be necessary to provide for the transport of the sick.

The expeditionary corps of Madagascar had 4 campaign hospitals, of 250 beds each; 1 hospital of evacuation, of 500 beds; 2 flying field hospitals and 13 field hospital infirmaries. There was also a sanitarium of 500 beds.

The field hospitals were provided with a considerable number of dressing materials, hand-litters, horse-litters, and *cacolets*.

The *matériel* of the unit of the sanitary organizations—the battalion service—included 2 Lefebvre wagons; 11 pack-mules; 10 paniers of supplies, 2 medical, 2 operating, 2 of dressings and quinine; 10 field-hospital bags; 12 litters, with hoods; and 1 conical tent.

Each body was to be followed in its operations by a field hospital comprising 12 Lefebvre wagons, 8 pack-mules, 10 mules for *cacolets*, 2 mules for litters, and a suitable number of coolies.

A road had been supposed to exist; the regulation wagons for a field hospital had been replaced by the Lefebvre; the horse-litters and *cacolets* reserved for mountain warfare were provided; and a great number of bearers was counted on; finally, the provisions for the wounded were calculated as in European war; but the medicines, except the quinine, were far from being sufficient.

The four campaign hospitals were each provided with 72 wagons, mules, supplies of all kinds, tents and barracks in sections.

In short, the supplies were abundant, and yet the campaign was bad, because there was a defective organization.

In the colonies the sick should not be kept on the spot, especially in a new country; the evacuation should be prompt, and what is needed for the first aid is a simple system of supply, divided into fractions, manageable, and easily transported.

As to the medical *matériel*, the heavy bottle-cases should be replaced by wicker paniers, closed by strong straps, and covered with water-proof. Each panier has rope handles, through which are passed the bamboos of the coolie bearers. Such is the improvised panier which of late years has served our colleagues in Dahomey and Indo-China.

Paniers of this kind are regulation in the Department of War, and it would be desirable to have a special model, well provided with compartments, adopted for all the colonial battalions and regiments.

These paniers could be stored in each important post, and at the moment of mobilization every surgeon could take the field with his sanitary *matériel*. This *matériel* should be prepared in advance and kept complete, or completed at the last moment in accordance with any special requirements. There should be no necessity of hastily drawing from bottle-cases or from the pharmacy. Paniers prepared in such a manner are sure to be badly composed.

The pharmaceutical *matériel* should be appropriate to the uses and necessities of the locality. It is not advisable in Tong-King, for example, to allow a column to start out without a sufficient supply of laudanum, quinine, and root of ipecac, for those attacked by diarrhœa, dysentery, or other pernicious disease.

The composition and number of paniers to distribute to each unit and to the sanitary organizations leaving Europe on an expedition should be studied and regulated in advance, and in a special manner for each expedition. To attain this end, the special nature of the expedition, its difficulties, and its duration must be known.

Doctor Fruitet is of the opinion that the regimental supplies of Europe can be utilized with certain modifications:

1. Suppress the regimental medical carriage.
2. Utilize only the collection of four paniers.
3. Suppress the two reserve paniers of dressings and replace them by medicine paniers.

The colonial and post store-houses should contain mobilization *matériel*; each of our colonies should be provided with a *matériel* suited to its needs.

If a great expedition were about to take place, it would only be necessary to call attention, in France, to the models and systems already in use in the colony, in order to prepare, in suitable proportions, the medical *matériel* needed by the columns.

MEANS OF TRANSPORT FOR THE SICK.

The mode of transport to adopt for the sick and wounded has its importance. There can be no question here of the luxurious conveyances and sanitary trains which usually accompany our European armies.

In the hot countries, the sick can best be conveyed to the hospitals in boats or junks or by transportation on the backs of animals or upon litters.

Boats are used only when the distance is long. In Tong-King, use is made of junks so arranged as to shelter the sick and wounded from the sun and rain. In Madagascar, there were lighters and steamers with which to descend the Betsiboka; they would have been more suitable if there had been a roof and curtains of blue muslin to prevent reverberation.

Transport on the backs of animals is not to be recommended. In France, in mountain warfare, mules and horses furnished with *cacolets* are used. This mode of transport is painful for the wounded, and is consequently not very practical; it can be used only for a certain class of sick, upon suitable roads, and for short journeys. It constitutes a veritable torture, under the sun, in countries which have no roads.

In the colonial wars, oxen, camels, and even elephants, have been employed; the objection to these is even more serious. In the Madagascar campaign, it was thought for a moment of using zebus, the native humped oxen. These animals are very numerous on the island; but it would have been necessary to train them to carry the pack, and the training would have taken several months of patient work. At Majunga, some of these zebus were trained to pull wagons, and even this operation was not without danger.

Beasts of burden can be properly used only in the transportation of rations and *matériel*; other means must be found for the sick.

The *transport on the back of man* is the most practical and comfortable for suffering men. It is performed with the aid of litters, hand-barrows, chairs, palanquins constructed in the fashion of the country, etc., constituting a very light and easily managed *matériel*.

The regulation war litter is not very practical for sloping ground; moreover, the handles are too short and the bearers, when they have to make a rather long journey, are obliged to add two handles of bamboo in order to obtain a longer lever-arm.

A good model is the palanquin used in Tong-King. In principle it is composed of a net suspended by its two extremities from a long bamboo; the natives placed at the ends carry it upon their shoulders; a sort of carapace, or covering, placed above the bamboo, protects the recumbent man from inclemencies.

The Dutch have improved on the palanquin and have adopted what they call the Chinese hand-barrow. It is made of a piece of sail-canvas 2 meters long, at the end of which are iron rods intended to keep the canvas stretched. Each rod has a ring at the center. A large bamboo 4 to 5 meters long is passed through the two rings, which are fastened and cannot approach each other. At each extremity of the handle is placed a piece of hollowed bamboo, supporting a matting roof to shelter the wounded.

In Dahomey, litters and hammocks were the principal modes of transport for the wounded. The hammock for two bearers, the one most employed, was composed of a bamboo of sufficient length, about 2.5 meters, and a material of cotton or canvas in the form of a ship hammock; the natives placed the extremities of the staffs upon their heads, and could thus complete a course of 6 kilometers an hour. The hammock for four bearers, more comfortable for the sick, was a sort of bamboo frame, provided with cotton cloth.

In Madagascar, the mode of transport commonly employ is the *filanzane*. This is a sort of palanquin carried by four men. The apparatus is light and easily managed. It is formed by wooden staves, each 3.3 meters in length, kept apart to a distance of only 34 centimeters by two cross-bars of iron. An iron frame, having a horizontal part for the seat and a curved part for the back, is fixed upon uprights of wood. The bottom of the frame is made of cloth; a little movable plank suspended by cords supports the feet.

The *filanzane* is a very practical apparatus and is easily procured in Madagascar. It was used for carrying the sick to the sanitarium of Nossi-Comba. The *bourjanes* or Malagasy bearers make great use of this system; they place the extremities of the wooden bars on their shoulders and almost always take a lengthened trot; they relieve each other without stopping, changing shoulders without difficulty, and make 4 kilometers an hour in a mountainous country.

The model in use by the Malagasies would be suitable as it is for carrying a convalescent. For the seriously sick and severely wounded, it would answer with a few very simple modifications: a greater separation of the staves, the addition of a hood to give protection from the sun or the rain, and the placing of a bamboo center to support the thighs and permit the wounded to lie down, with the lower limbs well supported upon this inclined plane.

Whatever the system adopted, it should not be forgotten to provide a great many of the transport apparatus. Considering the number of sick that may have to be provided for, we believe a general-in-chief ought to make sure of having a litter for every ten men, at least, to which should be attached two or four bearers.

In Dahomey, in spite of all the precautions taken, it was

necessary to hastily manufacture litters of fortune with branches of trees and the canvas of tents. An army of 5000 men, going under fire, ought to have 2000 coolies and 500 litters for the special service of sanitary convoy.

HOSPITALIZATION OF THE SICK AND WOUNDED.

Without counting the field hospitals and infirmaries where the sick and wounded receive first aid, but where they cannot remain for a long time, there is a choice between three great systems of hospitalization: the campaign hospitals, the hospital-ships, and the sanitaria. They answer to different needs, and should lend a mutual coöperation; in place of a regrettable antagonism, it is indispensable that there be complete harmony in the services.

1. *Campaign Hospitals.*

Whenever the operations are in the interior, it is necessary to establish campaign hospitals. The field hospital of the first line advances with the troops, and sometimes, when the distance is considerable, it is useful to connect it, by a field hospital of the second line, with the infirmary of the garrison, or, better still, with the campaign hospital which is to receive the seriously sick and wounded.

There should be no waiting for these hospitals to be made ready, and in consequence the necessary elements to establish them must be provided in advance.

Hutting might answer, in spite of the many complaints which have been made about the use of huts in colonial expeditions.

The hut is a defective lodging, often bad. If necessary to erect huts, they should always be built on the double-shell principle. To compensate for the slight thickness of the walls, they should be doubled: double walls, double ceiling, double floor, inclosing between their two surfaces a cushion of isolated air.

There are several models in our country. By choosing one possessing the desirable elements, bearing in mind the principle just laid down, it would be easy to erect a kind suitable for this purpose.

It might be possible to utilize certain of those light constructions, made for our temperate country, and too sensible to cosmical action by reason of their delicate texture, for use in the Tropics. On that account they might be placed under great sheds, whose roofs of boards or straw would shelter them from the rain, the sun, and the humidity. These roofs should project all around the walls of the hut, thus making a circular gallery, which could be inclosed, putting numerous doors and windows in the wall. This would also make a habitation with double walls, rapidly prepared, at little expense, and with all the advantages.

Tents are sometimes employed, but they are still more inconvenient. The shelter-tent, open upon three sides and arranged so as to form a horizontal roof and a posterior wall, neither protects from reverberation nor from the wind.

Equally objectionable are all the closed tents, conical or others, whose walls prevent proper ventilation.

A new condition is imposed for colonial campaigns. The most simple model to be recommended is one approaching the tent used upon the deck of ships. It consists of a large tarpaulin, stretched upon four pickets, with side curtains capable of being raised or lowered at will. The material could be made water-proof on the exterior and colored in green or blue. The ideal would be to have it double. It could be sprinkled in the hot hours of the day to cool it and could be carefully covered with foliage.

The Madagascar campaign showed the defectiveness of all these systems. The tents, while easy to set up, were uninhabitable; the temperature under the great tent of the hospital at Suburbieville rose to 38 degrees at the bedside of the sick and to 42 degrees between the two canvases. The huts adopted were of the Werhlin-Espitalier system; the walls were made of a trellis of iron wire and cocoa hair; the roof of canvas. The Malagasy constructions, of raphia, well raised above the ground, with a double roof and wall and a gallery, were the most satisfactory hygienically; they were to be preferred to all the others.

The greatest trouble with improvised hospitals is to provide all the accessories. The hospital at Majunga was organized after a time; it consisted of board huts, Espitalier huts, and tents of all kinds; the sick were passably quartered, but the kitchen was in the open air, the water failed, the sink-screens left much to be desired, and disinfection was impossible.

The hospitals were scarcely established before they were overflowing; each was intended to receive 250 men, and they soon had to shelter 600 and more. At Ankaboka, where the hospital of evacuation was located, there was an unheard-of crowding of sick. Coolies mixed with European soldiers were crowded there. It was useless to give the natives beds which they would not use; huts with a sort of camp bed and bedding would have sufficed for them; there they would have found more comfort and infection would have been less great.

Even in Europe, disease has always been the great enemy of armies in campaign. In colonial wars this enemy is still more formidable. That is why too great pains cannot be taken to provide the means capable of insuring the proper care of the sick.

This is an approved doctrine in ordinary times; yet everybody seems to be ignorant of it when an expedition is about to be undertaken.

2. *Hospital-Ships.*

As soon as possible the sick should be withdrawn from the usually defective campaign hospitals and placed upon hospital-ships, held as near as possible to the base of operations.

For a long time and with reason it has been the idea to use ships for quartering and caring for the sick in the expeditions to the paludal countries of the torrid zone.

In 1841, at the time of the Nossi-Bé expedition, the mortality diminished greatly from the time the soldiers of the expeditionary corps were required to go aboard the ships every evening. Observations of the same kind were made in Madagascar during the campaign of 1884-1885; the fever never left the men quartered on land; a sojourn aboard could alone relieve them of it.

This conviction undoubtedly existed in the mind of the superior authority when it was decided, at the beginning of the expedition of 1895, to send to Majunga the great hospital-transport *Shamrock*, the direction of which was confided to Doctor Burot, chief surgeon of Marine.

Placing in the bay of Bombetoke an admirably regulated hospital-ship, with all the means for assuring the well-being of the sick, was not one of the least services rendered by the Marine to the expeditionary corps. And it is one of the measures which has been received with most favor, since it answered the unanimous prayer: *Protect our soldiers from the fever.*

It can be affirmed that many lives would have been spared if the troops, from their arrival, while awaiting the preparations and the march to the front, had been quartered upon the water and hospitalized upon the ships. It is indispensable, in undertaking the conquest of a fever country where nothing has been prepared, to have floating barracks for quartering the men, at least at night, and hospital-ships to care for the sick.

What a Hospital-Ship Ought to Be.—It is especially in colonial expeditions that the need of the veritable hospital-ship makes itself felt; but a vessel which is to remain in a roadstead to receive the sick and care for them ought to be regulated differently from one intended for their transport to the mother-country.

It is to be regretted that, before its departure from France, the *Shamrock*, hastily equipped, could not have received new installations and that it was impossible to provide an organization compatible with the service to be performed. It seems that we had lost sight of the example of the *Victor-Emanuel*, at the Gold Coast, and also of the recommendation made twenty years ago by Admiral Ryder, to follow that model whenever it was necessary to prepare a new hospital-ship.

The English, before sending the *Victor-Emanuel* to Cape Coast, made some material modifications. All had been seen and calculated for the welfare of the sick. A roof, on a level with the poop, transformed the deck into a supplementary broadside. Movable planking was put in for renewing the air, platforms for promenading in the open air, beds for certain classes of wounds, ice-houses, and improved ventilating apparatus.*

---

*During the last campaign against the Ashantees, in 1896-97, the English fitted up the *Coromandel* in a remarkable manner. Having chartered this superb steamer of 4800 tons from the Peninsular and Oriental Company, they transformed it into a luxurious hospital, furnished most suitably: a day salon, protected from the sun by a double roof and movable Venetian blinds, an isolation ward, an operating-room, a steam apparatus for ventilation between decks, punkas and fans moved by steam, electric lights, improved laundry, disinfection and distillation apparatus, machines for making seltzer-water and ice, cold-storage room for preserving meat, milk, and

The crew lived forward and was separated from the sick, never communicating with them. A special place was reserved for convalescents; the hospital service was absolutely distinct from that of the ship. Doctor Beckley, having eight surgeons under his orders and a large number of assistants, directed and administered the hospital in a thorough manner; he decided as to the repatriation of the men, the measures of sanitation or isolation, and the transport of the wounded.

At Massonah, the Italians transformed an old transport, the *Garibaldi*, into a hospital. The deck was made into a great hospital ward; there were large port-holes everywhere and well-regulated private wards. Two hulks were attached to the ship, on one of which distilled water was prepared, and on the other, ice—not only for the hospital, but for the whole garrison.

At Souakim, in 1884, the *Orontes* became a hospital of 300 beds; the *Ganges*, in 1885, played the same *rôle*.

With the Dutch, also, during the second expedition against Atjeh, the *Filips-Van-Marnix* served as a hospital. This ship was under the direct orders of a chief surgeon, and Van Leent informs us that there was nothing but praise for this organization.

In France, we are far from attaining this end; but we could at least, without reference to the source of authority, make some little advance. We would say that in order to usefully fulfill its *rôle*, the *Shamrock* should have been *specialized*; like the *Melville* at Hong-Kong, it should have been a hospital-ship and nothing else.

It cannot be admitted that a ship intended to receive a

---

vegetables, an electric kitchen, and inodorous closets with automatic flush.

The *Coromandel* astonished all the surgeons who visited her. She was unused, on account of the rapidity of the campaign and of the hygienic measures which had been taken.

great number of sick is adapted at the same time to the transport of troops and above all of animals, to become a store-house for supplies, and serve as a prison or insane asylum. In place of being a barracks where military drills are carried on, it ought to be a place of repose where all useless noises are suppressed.

Specialization is the Law of Progress.—This principle, unfortunately, is not sufficiently applied. Yet, everywhere, everybody feels that it is difficult to do several things at the same time. On arriving at Majunga, a portion of the *personnel* should have been disembarked, reducing it to a minimum sufficient to assure the service of the ship's boats, the manufacture of soft water and of bread, cleanliness, and discipline.

An effective strength of 120 men, in place of 300, would have been an economy, and, as a consequence, there would have been a greater number of beds. In these conditions, the *Shamrock* could have received 500 sick in a permanent manner.

The great advantage of the system was the immediate utilization of a hospital in working order the same day of its arrival. To appreciate this it was only necessary to see the difficulties experienced in establishing the hospital at Majunga. With unheard-of efforts, accommodations for 500 men were prepared after a considerable time; but to attain this result it was necessary to have recourse to tents, which had the inconvenience (especially the conical tents) of being too hot in the day-time and too cold at night.

The number of beds was insufficient for the large number of sick; they were supplemented by litters placed directly on the ground, which exposed the men anew to paludal attack and rendered the pernicious accesses more frequent and more formidable.

There was a deficiency of water; the quantity was not sufficient for laundry purposes, nor even for the bodily cleanliness of the men, who could not wash themselves and remained for a long time covered with dirt and dust.

The military health service was very quickly overrun, not being able to multiply itself beyond measure.

What we have just said proves again that the sea hospitals are the best at the beginning of an expedition. They permit the hospital arrangements on shore to be properly made and completed.

The need at Madagascar was a stationary floating hospital, almost dismantled, with hulks as annexes, and two great transports to repatriate the sick.*

The Shamrock at Majunga.—The *Shamrock* was given a special *personnel*: a chief surgeon, a surgeon of the 1st class, a surgeon of the 2d class, a pharmacist of the 2d class, and ten nurses. It was provided with all the necessary *matériel* in the way of medicines, dressings, and instruments. From this point of view nothing was lacking.

First of all, Admiral Bienaimé, the commander-in-chief of the naval division of the Indian Ocean, took a number of energetic measures.

The *Shamrock* was to receive only Europeans, to the exclusion of the natives. It is evident that the European and Algerian troops were especially entitled to benefit from the advantages of a nautical habitation. The natives pay little

---

*During the Dahomey expedition, in 1892, the *Mytho*, anchored at Kotonou, served quite extensively as a hospital for the sick of the expeditionary corps. During the period of active operations, from August to December, 1892, it hospitalized 528 sick, of whom 436 were fever patients and 92 wounded. As a general rule, the wounded were cared for on land and the fever patients on the *Mytho*. This was a wise arrangement; in fact, it may be a difficult matter in certain cases to remove a wounded man to a great distance and place him upon a ship. In 1885, the *Nive*, the *Annamite*, and the *Tong-King* served as floating hospitals for the squadron of Admiral Courbet in the China seas.

attention to cleanliness and may become a source of contamination; it is better to keep them on land and together, giving them mats or camp beds and bedding.

The kinds of diseases had also to be considered.

If paludism in all its forms is advantageously modified by the sea climate, it is not the same with certain other affections, like tuberculosis and rheumatism, which are not aggravated by a sojourn on land.

The contagious diseases, variola, measles, typhoid fever, can not be conveniently treated on board, because isolation is difficult when there is no vessel as an annex.

The sick, upon admission, after having been examined and registered, were conducted, when possible, to the bathroom, where their bodily cleanliness was attended to. Moreover, the cleanliness of the sick was an object of special attention. Means of ablution were placed at their disposal.

All the effects of the sick were passed through the disinfecting apparatus; the shoes and other objects of leather, not being able to support the humid heat without deteriorating, were disinfected by the sublimate with the aid of a large atomizer. Twice a week the decks of the hospital were gone over with potash and washed with chloride of zinc; the same for the walls and for the iron and wood portions of the beds.

At each departure, the mattress and bedding were passed through the disinfecting stove. Whenever there was a death in a room, the place was hermetically sealed and fumigated with sulphur for twenty-four hours; an atomizer with the sublimate was then used in all parts of the room, which was repainted, while the bedding was disinfected by vapor under pressure.

The laundry, working regularly, permitted the cleaning of all the soiled linen. The hygienic buckets always contained disinfectants.

The sick were well nourished and the meals as varied as possible. The ration of the sick, made up according to medical prescriptions, had as its base the ration aboard: bread, meat, beans, coffee, and sugar; in addition, there were commodities specially embarked for the sick, and finally, there was bought on the spot, to replace the commodities embarked, any thing which could improve the mess.

The general recapitulation of the foods dispensed in the hospital of the *Shamrock* was scrupulously made. The calculations were made for each commodity separately.

The food on the *Shamrock*, in regard to variety and preparation, was equal to that of a great hospital in France, and yet, taking everything into account, each patient was fed at a rate of 1 fr. 37 per day.

It would be interesting to consider the cost price of the ration for the patient in a campaign hospital, and establish the comparison.

The soldiers all wanted to go to the *Shamrock*, and some of them considered themselves saved when they saw their names on the removal list. They would no more be put to bed on the ground, in the dust, and they knew they would find what was necessary.

Results of the Campaign.—The results of the campaign are easy to appreciate.

From the day of the departure from Toulon, the 27th of January, 1895, to the day of return, the 15th of September, of the same year, in eight months and fifteen days, there were 63 deaths on board. From this number it is necessary to deduct 3, pertaining to the crew or to sailors embarked for subsistence.

The *Shamrock* having really commenced its service as a hospital-ship only in the month of March, there remain 60 deaths for a period of six months, among the men received as patients: this gives 10 deaths per month, or 1 every three days. This proportion is not comparable to that of the same epoch in the campaign hospitals, at Majunga and especially at Ankaboka; it approaches, moreover, though it is inferior to, that usually observed in the hospitals of Toulon and Saint-Mandrier.

In the 60 are included not only the deaths which took place at Majunga while the ship was stationed there, but also those which took place during the return voyage, and which considerably increase the proportion.

The sanitary condition of the *Shamrock* may be looked at from two different standpoints. In the five months from the 15th of March to the 15th of August, there were 20 deaths; in one month, from the 15th of August to the 15th of September, there were 40. The proportion at departure from Majunga had been 1.5 per cent; the return voyage raised it to 3 per cent.

During the entire period of six months the *Shamrock* received 2000 sick; there was a daily average of 300, giving 46,000 hospital days.

Relatively, the total number of 60 deaths for such a large number of sick, and under such exceptional circumstances, is of a nature to inspire reflection.

In August, the sanitary situation had become very critical in Madagascar, and, if the transports were put to the sad necessity of throwing many cadavers into the sea, it was chiefly because the sick were in a state of intense cachexy when they were embarked. It is to be regretted that the repatriation did not commence sooner.

After what took place on the unhealthy banks of the Betsiboka, there is no doubt but that the campaign hospitals would have been advantageously replaced by ships, hulks, or lighters, anchored at different points of the river. The military surgeons were devoted; they accomplished their duty with the greatest intelligence, but they could not shelter their sick from the effluvia of the marshes. In the course of the campaign, everybody regretted not having had several floating hospitals; some stationary, to receive all the sick of the expeditionary corps; others mobile, to conduct them to the sanitaria or to France.

3. *Sanitaria.*

In colonial campaigns, there has been a thought of using certain localities, favored as to situation and altitude, in order to send there, upon their departure from the hospitals, the sick, or rather the convalescents, in the hope that, after a few weeks of repose, they might be able to rejoin the column. It is principally in Madagascar that this has been tried.

In 1884, places of convalescence had been sought on the East Coast. The results were bad, none of the places chosen having fulfilled the conditions of a veritable sanitarium. The island of Reunion, thirty hours from Tamatave, was tried for the purpose, and then abandoned because it did not render the services expected. Men were sent back to Madagascar, after a short sojourn at Saint-Denis, who were seriously affected by paludism. Reunion could then have rendered real service, but on the express condition of serving as a place of transition between Madagascar and France, for the paludal patients who were no more to be sent to the great Malagasy Island.

Before the campaign of 1895, the creation of a sanitarium was decided upon; various locations had been proposed and the Minister of War had sent a commission to study the question upon the spot. The island of Anjouan presented certain advantages; Mount d'Ambre had its partisans. Nossi Comba was selected, and, in our opinion, was the best place.

In choosing Nossi-Comba, the delegates of the Minister of War conformed to the recommendations of several of our colleagues of the Marine. Nossi-Comba is only an hour by boat from Hell-Ville, capital of the colony of Nossi-Bé, provided with alimentary resources and upon the route of the regular packet-boats. To come from Majunga, twenty-four hours suffice by a sea always calm, well sheltered by the central ridge of Madagascar. The disembarkation of the sick is easy; there is an excellent anchorage for large vessels in a little roadstead partially circumscribed by islets.

The island of Nossi-Comba, formed of two cones in juxtaposition, is relatively healthy; it is not marshy. There is a sandy beach and sloping ground, which facilitates natural drainage. Shade is found there, and the sea breezes, blowing from the north in the morning and the south in the afternoon, maintain a beneficial ventilation.

The establishment was constructed at an altitude of 480 meters above the level of the sea, upon a crest transformed by the care of the engineers. Unfortunately, it was necessary to remove the soil from great surfaces in order to level the site and erect the hutting. The consequences, always the same in these regions, did not delay in making themselves felt by the soldier-workmen.

The constructions of the sanitarium comprised: 1. Huttings of the type adopted by the administration, with frames of iron (Werhlin-Espitalier system) of two models; one, a veritable shed, a sick ward for the men; the other, a little more comfortable, for the use of the officers. 2. Large wooden huts built in the fashion of the country and also intended for the use of the sick. 3. Annexes and local accessories of the same construction, but without boards.

The Werhlin-Espitalier huts presented some inconveniences which it will be useful to point out. The hinged sheet-iron used as a roof absorbed an enormous quantity of heat, which was reflected to the inside, the more so as these huts have no ceiling. They were not sufficiently elevated above the ground; there was no floor under the gallery serving as a place of promenade and as a dining-room. Finally, the soil had been excavated for the construction of the platforms upon which they were built. Thus the nurses and the sappers of the engineers were attacked by fevers, born upon the spot, according to the testimony of the distinguished chief surgeon of the sanitarium, Doctor Malinas, himself.

The huts constructed by the local administration in the Malagasy fashion did not have these inconveniences, and presented other advantages besides.

Composed of an immense floor of mangrove, supported by pillars of the same material, the height of which above the ground varied according to the declivity, they were 6 meters high under the ridge parallel to the median and longitudinal axis of the floor. On each side, the exterior portion of a double inclined plane formed the gallery. This roof, supported by mangrove trunks joined together by wooden traverses, had a skeleton with strong ribs of raphia, covered by very regularly imbricated leaves of the ranevala. Under this sort of shed was placed the hut proper, serving as a ward for the sick.

These huts were very cool, bathed on all sides by air and light. The ventilation was chiefly provided by four doors, two on each of the long sides and opposite those on the other side, but ventilation was also provided in an insensible manner through the interstices of the walls. At the two extremities of the shed, the triangular gable was likewise covered with ranevala leaves, imbricated, in order to prevent the entrance of the oblique rays of the rising and setting sun.

This proves once more the advantage of knowing the

resources of the country where one is established and which it is a question of utilizing. Enormous expense of transport and material are avoided; one goes faster and does better. At all times and in all places the surgeons of the expeditionary columns have preferred, to the barracks in sections, the constructions of fortune judiciously disposed, according to the resources and the fashion of the country in which the operations have taken place.

The bedding comprised 250 iron bedsteads with springs and mattresses, and 250 bed-litters, of the Strauss system, for convalescents.

The water, coaxed from various sources, was of good quality and was nearly sufficient; but it was necessary to establish a system of canals and to construct reservoirs. On two different occasions the delivery diminished in a manner to cause uneasiness.

The supplies came from Nossi-Bé. The road, laid out by the engineers along an old path, was 4 kilometers in length, but, owing to its grade, was impassable for wagons. Thus the commodities necessary for food were brought each morning on the backs of men.

If the inconveniences to which the higher altitude would expose the men had been known in advance, other dispositions would certainly have been made. It would have been useful, according to the proposition of Admiral Bienaimé, to locate a first hospital at Ampangourine, upon the border of the sea, at the very point of disembarkation, in a situation as agreeable as healthy. There, those sent from the other hospitals could have lived, and only the convalescents, the anaemics, would have been sent to the heights.

At Nossi-Comba the nights were cool and damp; in July it was 26 to 28 degrees during the day and 16 to 18 degrees during the night. Beginning at 6 o'clock in the evening, there was a mist, and in the morning, at reveille, everything was covered with dew.

The attacks of fever there were less frequent than at Majunga; but, as is the rule under the circumstances, diarrhœas were more numerous; rheumatism and tuberculosis patients did not do well there.

The hope of sending the men back to the column after treatment was delusive. In reality, Nossi-Comba was restricted to use as a station between Madagascar and the ships charged with repatriation. It was no longer anæmics more or less worn out by the hot climate, who came there in search of health, but men heavily depressed by attacks of a formidable paludism and whom it was important to shelter as quickly as possible from danger by sending them back to France.

If the mountainous climates in the tropical regions have an incontestible advantage as a means of preservation from paludal diseases, they present dangers which should be well known when it is proposed to establish a sanitarium, the object of which, in a hot country, is very different from what one is accustomed to believe it in Europe.

In 1895, in Japan, at Nagasaki, Admiral de Beaumont, commanding the naval division of the Extrême-Orient, had the happy idea of renting, upon the heights which dominate the magnificent roadstead, a country-house belonging to a religious congregation, in order to send there for convalescence, in September and October, a certain number of sailors of the naval division, who had been attacked by cholera and the paludal fevers of Woosung. It was agreed that, according to roster, one of the surgeons of the ships present in the roadstead should go twice a week to Tomachi to visit the convalescents. *No man whose condition demanded medical care was to be sent* to the sanitarium. The establishment was to furnish excellent food.

All the paludal patients sent under these conditions to Tomachi recovered rapidly and were able to rejoin their ships completely cured. On the contrary, there were relapses among the former diarrhœa patients, which necessitated their repatriation.

Diarrhœa, dysentery, and hepatitis do not disappear in the heights of the tropical countries; far from it, they reappear. The dampness and the coolness of the nights provoke their reappearance, and also that of paludal attacks in the case of persons who commit the slightest imprudence.

The tendency to diarrhœa is so marked that several English surgeons have written that the diarrhœa of the mountains is only a transformation of the malaria, which in inferior regions produces the attack of fever. It is sure, however, that this diarrhœa of the heights quickly produces an anaemic condition; it has a cachectical influence like scurvy. It is ameliorated neither by medicine nor diet; repatriation alone, the sea-voyage, can restore the blood of the sick to its normal condition, if there is yet time.

So, if the altitudes prevent, they do not cure; the sanitaria of hot countries should never be hospitals, but simply places of waiting for the convalescents to be repatriated; in the nautical habitation, the hospital-ship specially prepared, there is health for the paludal patients whose cure is still possible.

Experience has always and everywhere demonstrated the excellence of this system, and in Madagascar, before the expedition, everybody was of this opinion. The operations once begun, it was too late; the utilization of the enormous *matériel* sent from France obtruded itself.

Contrary to current ideas and to the interpretations which have been given to the *rôle* of a sanitarium, the figures furnished by the hospital of Tamatave confirm what we have just said.

From the 12th of December, 1894, the day of the arrival of the troops, to the 20th of February, 1896, the day of the raising of the state of siege in Madagascar, 673 men were sent from Tamatave to the various sanitary establishments of Reunion. In the case of these 673, who all presented slightly accentuated symptoms of malarial impregnation, we observe the following: 10 died at Reunion; 232 were directly repatriated; 167 were kept in service in the island; 142 remained under treatment until the 20th of February, 1896; 122 only were judged capable of returning to Madagascar.

In short, 18 per cent of the number were able to rejoin; but if we follow these 122 men, we can judge what they were worth. In the six months following their return, 2 died; 7 creoles had to be sent again to their country, Reunion; 32 were repatriated as sick; only 81 lasted more than six months, but they furnished such a number of days on the sick-report that their services may be considered as having been practically worthless.

We are of the opinion of Doctor Robert, when he says that early repatriation would have been more efficacious and less burdensome. The hospitals of Reunion have been of service only in preparing for repatriation some of the sick who would probably have died if they had been put directly *en route* to France. The sanitaria are not, and never will be, more than waiting hospitals; this should be remembered in our future colonial expeditions.

EVACUATIONS.

All men who have been seriously affected by the climate should be returned to the mother-country, if they are able to stand a sea-voyage.

The English have set us the example at the Gold Coast, in repatriating their sick; we had reason to imitate them in Dahomey, in 1890 and 1892. "Once the organism is attacked, once the long drama of intoxication is commenced." M. L. Colin has said, "the wiser it is to have recourse, when possible, to an absolute and positive prophylactic remedy: repatriation. This is why we send back to France, from Rome, so many of our soldiers, who, once attacked, would run not only all the risks of frequent and sometimes mortal relapses, but who, besides, by reason of their progressive weakening, would become completely unfit for the exigencies of the military service."

For fever patients, the greatest danger is to continue to live in the atmosphere which has poisoned them. Experience has shown that repatriation at an opportune time almost always results in rapid recovery from fevers. No doubt, some might have the fever in France; pernicious attacks might even be presented there, the development precipitated by a brusque change of climate; this frequently causes pneumonia, always serious for cachectics. These individual accidents cannot be invoked against a general measure, the more so since they are equally formidable in the higher altitudes of the sanitaria.

France has always been, and always will be, the best place of convalescence for our colonial soldiers.

In an expedition like that of Madagascar, it is not sufficient to provide for sending the sick of the column to the coast; it is necessary to have from the beginning a service of evacuation to France. The true hospital of evacuation ought to be a ship carrying all the sick judged useless to the expeditionary corps.

There should have been organized, at the commencement of operations, a system of rapid evacuation from Majunga to Algiers, Toulon, and Marseilles. It was due to the tenacity of M. Emery-Desprousses, surgeon inspector, that a solution in this sense was arrived at, unfortunately, a little late, and only when the director of the health service of the expeditionary corps had no more trouble in demonstrating, by the deaths daily recorded in Madagascar, that repatriation was the only chance for safety.

Once more it may be said that a sojourn in the temporary hospitals on land upon a marshy coast cannot cure the fever. Moreover, every sick and wounded man entering one of them, whatever the nature of his affection, is exposed to contract the fever.

A colonial expedition commences in France and ends there; that is to say, the important duties of forwarding the *personnel* and *matériel*, and of the repatriation and continued evacuation of the sick, are intimately connected with the operations. It may be affirmed that the success of the enterprise is determined upon the water, upon the sea, as well as upon the territory to which we carry our arms, and that the military and hygienic success of the campaign depends upon the proper working of this double service: on the one hand, the forwarding of elements new and serviceable; and on the other hand, the elimination of elements worn out. Only the military or *militarized* services are capable of properly carrying out such a programme.

That is why the Minister of Marine will always have, independently of the military *rôle* of the war fleet, very grave obligations and very heavy burdens in case of a colonial expedition; and, in our opinion, this is not the least reason which ought to militate in favor of keeping the colonial troops in the department to which they belong to-day.

Public opinion was aroused in France by seeing those repatriated from Madagascar and by learning the number of deaths which had taken place *en route*. The emotion was quickly calmed when it was learned what had taken place in the island itself.

While 600 men died in the hospitals on land, an average of 4 per day, the deaths on the transports averaged only 2 per day.

With an equal number of sick in the same condition, the deaths on the voyage were only half as great, and those who arrived in France had many more chances of recovery, for the supreme hope of the sick soldier was to see again his native land.

If the repatriation had begun in April, the men would not have arrived at the degree of anæmia which they presented in the following months. Those repatriated on the *Shamrock* came partly from the hospital of Ankaboka; they were in a lamentable state when they embarked; their faces were pale and swollen, their intelligence extinguished, their limbs half paralyzed. On the evening of the day of their arrival, several died suddenly. Very evidently it was not the embarkation which killed them, but cachexy. Logical conclusion: embarked sooner, they would not have died.

Repatriation was then indicated; it should have been speedily ordered and surrounded by certain supplementary guaranties. The sanitaria, which could not cure, would have been able to keep the seriously sick and prepare the others for the journey; that is to say, clean them, clothe them, cheer them up, and send them aboard only when in a condition to support the voyage.

The isolation dépôt at Majunga should have furnished articles of clothing to each soldier about to be repatriated; issues of soap and tobacco should have been made to each man, either from the subsistence supplies, or from the gifts of the patriotic aid societies. This was only partially done. Thanks to the societies, whose aid has been so useful, the soldiers were at least provided with warm clothing.

The dangerous phase of repatriation at that time was

the crossing of the Red Sea, as is almost always the case, considering the situation of our colonies. It is, above all, a question of season; when the sun is highest—in September, for example—the voyage is the most to be feared. In the hottest seasons, it is chiefly when one lands during the outward voyage that one suffers most. The frequent breeze from the north often makes the return voyage easier to bear. With ships of great speed, at least 15 knots, the progress of the vessel facilitates the aëration of the inhabited quarters. They should therefore be given the preference and stops at Djibouti and Aden should be avoided, as they are more distressing than the voyage itself.*

Variations of temperature are not less to be feared. On entering the Red Sea in summer, the thermometer suddenly jumps from 20 to 35 and 40 degrees, where it remains during the crossing, and then descends again to about 20 degrees on leaving the canal.

Advanced cachectics are inadequate to the gymnastics imposed by this temperature on their lungs and skin.

On the whole, in bad conditions of sojourn, especially when confronted by paludism, repatriation, cost what it may, is the only rational method of treatment, as M. L. Colin has said.

If the expeditionary corps in Madagascar had continued to remain in the valley of the Betsiboka, if it had not been decided a little later to repatriate, the army would have disappeared and the disaster would perhaps have surpassed that of San Domingo.

§ V. *Hygienic Conduct of Operations.*

Let us suppose that everything is prepared for an expe-

---

*In motion, there is always a little breeze; at anchor, there is none. Hospital-transports should be very fast in order to cross the dangerous zone as rapidly as possible, and they should have sufficient supplies to make it unnecessary to stop at intermediate ports.

dition and that the campaign begins; we are going to follow the soldier and give some more advice. Indeed, we must still examine the measures relative to the concentration of the troops at the base of operations, the march to the front, encamping, and hygiene.

CONCENTRATION.

After having chosen his troops, the chief will take the necessary steps to concentrate them at a point whence they can be put in march.

This concentration, and the whole campaign as well, should be made in the favorable season—that is, the dry season and also the cool season.

The operations should take place from October to April in Tong-King; from November to February in Cochin-China; from October to March in Senegal. At Bénin, on the contrary, it is necessary to act in the season of the high waters, from August to October, because the herbaceous vegetation will then have disappeared and this disappearance will permit of movement, while the state of the rivers will allow an easy access to the gun-boats.

It would be a great error to order an expedition at the moment when an epidemic has just broken out in the territory the troops would have to cross. The epidemic would find in the march of the columns a ready means of diffusion, and would not fail to levy a heavy mortuary tribute on the effectives.

During the period of concentration, care should be taken to avoid fatiguing the troops excessively, and especially to avoid marches which would exhaust them prematurely and result only in the inconvenience of a loss of much time. The sea or the rivers, *those roads which march*, should be utilized. The rapidity with which the transport and concentration of the units at the initial point is made, whether by despatch-boats, ship's boats, and tugs, or by simple junks and lighters, will be a condition of success.

It was a too slow concentration and a defective organization which seem to have produced the bad sanitary results of the campaign of Madagascar. While the *matériel* followed the water-way, all the troops marched painfully by land. It took them three months to reach Suberbieville, where they could have been transported in fifteen days, if all the disposable means had been employed. The fortified posts of the Hovas were echeloned along the river and accessible by the water-way. The *Gabès* and the *Boëni*, used by the commander in chief of the naval division, Admiral Bienaimé, to reconnoiter the river, would have been able to occupy Marohogo, Mevarana, and Maroway. The troops could have been transported by boat to within 25 kilometers of Suberbieville, and thus spared a march of 260 kilometers across the marshes. The concentration of men and *matériel* could have been made at Suberbieville; it was possible to push on as far as Andriba without making a road, and, after a second concentration, the column could have started, as it did, for Tamanarivo.

THE MARCH TO THE FRONT.

There is no doubt as to the result of fatigue imposed on soldiers campaigning in a pronounced paludal country like Senegal, the Soudan, or Madagascar. It may be said that each step of our columns towards the center of the Black Continent or towards the capital of l'Emyrne has been marked by a dead body.

The principal object of a corps commander, then, will be to husband the strength of his troops. The marches should be made during the least hot portions of the day. Their duration, broken by halts of ten minutes every hour, should be from three to five hours, at most, during which will be covered, according to the nature and necessities of the terrain, from 12 to 20 kilometers as a maximum. The troops should never be required to make a single march as great as 30 kilometers, except in case of absolute necessity.

In campaign, the marches should be so regulated that the men will not be exposed to paludal emanations. No going out before the rising or after the setting of the sun; no marching during the warm hours, which should be devoted to repose; two short intervals—one from six to nine o'clock in the morning, the other from four to six o'clock in the evening—ought to suffice.

With a view to avoiding the inconveniences of the fatigue imposed by the march in the hot countries, it has been suggested to mount the infantry. This was tried in the Soudan, and was acknowledged by everybody to have certainly contributed to the diminution of mortality among the European troops. The horse and the mule of Senegal are replaced in South Algeria by camels and dromedaries. In Cambodia, in 1885, elephants were utilized in default of other mount.

Unfortunately, circumstances will arise when the necessities of war will impose the formal obligation of lengthening the route, increasing the load, and forestalling or prolonging the hours propitious for the march. In this case, the greatest precautions, always useful, will be absolutely imperious.

The men should have breakfast immediately after reveille, before confronting the rays of the sun, *the enemy above*, and the emanations from the ground, *the enemy below*.

The ranks will be completely opened, in order not to transport parallel to the column a bed of air heated by bodily radiation. Troops in the hot countries rarely march in good order on account of the condition of the roads; Indian file is often the only disposition which can be adopted.

The clothing should be open; the outer clothing might be taken off and carried on the arms; the underclothing, however, should always be worn, as the heat of the sun on the unsheltered skin, like coolness, is always to be feared.

The poor marchers, placed at the head, will regulate the march and prevent a too rapid pace.

The canteens should be filled with coffee and water, with tea, or some acid drink. Stopping to drink or to draw water from the ponds encountered should be absolutely prohibited.

In case of rain, water may be caught in the water-proof stretched over the arms; this will also serve to protect the soldier.

Upon halting, it would be better to keep the men in the sun for a time than to place them immediately in the shade; the difference in temperature might be enough to chill them. For the same reason, even more here than on the march, the men should be positively forbidden to completely uncover themselves.

It would also be very imprudent to permit the men to lie on the ground in the sun. The reverberation and action of the heat reflected from a burning soil are the more to be feared the nearer the man's head is to the ground.

This is an observation made by all soldiers since General Bugeaud: in campaign in the hot countries, a man lying down will be more exposed to sun-stroke than a man on his knees; the latter, than a man standing; and this last, than a man on horseback, whose face is 2.4 meters from the ground.

During a fight, this data may be important for the sharp-shooters, who are often placed in these different positions.

If, in spite of all these precautions, a man should be sun-struck or overcome by the heat, he should be immediately placed under a shelter, improvised with all haste, with his head raised and well protected from the ground; the body and face should be bathed with cold water, his limbs should be stimulated by friction, and as soon as consciousness begins to return, he should be forced to drink in small draughts.

In case respiration should be suspended, artificial respiration will be resorted to by raising both arms of the patient above his head simultaneously and then lowering them along the body, about twenty times a minute; or, better still, by making rhythmical tractions of the tongue.

CAMPING.

No one is ignorant of the danger run by armies obliged to camp on unhealthful ground. During the occupation of Rome, the soldiers changing garrison were not lodged under tents upon their arrival at the halting-places; they were installed for the night in the granges, farms, sheds, and in all disposable places. This is preferable hygienically to any encampment whatever.

In fact, when an army traverses a fever country, if centers of population exist, it ought to be quartered upon the inhabitants and established in the houses with a view to avoiding a night either in bivouac or under a tent, which offers only an insufficient shelter from the ground and the mists. If there are no centers of habitation, ingenuity should be taxed to create shelters for the night.

In Algeria, our soldiers are accustomed to using the tent. This method of camping is so common, in fact, that each locality should have a camping-place for passing troops; when exceptional climatic conditions require, requisition is made for cantonments.

It should be known that in our tropical colonies the conditions are very different from those of Algeria, and that methods praised for the one place are not practical in the other.

If necessary to camp, the best system of tent should be used, improved, as far as possible, with branches and foliage.

The ground on which the camp is to be located should never be dug up, but only cleaned and prepared by fire. This will be the best way of driving away insects, destroying the brushwood, and calcining the ground, rendered thus impermeable.

As water is necessary for cleanliness and alimentation, the camp may prudently be established in proximity to a water-course, to the windward of marshes, and upon a relief of the terrain, if not upon an elevated place.

Without removing too much earth, trenches will be traced in the direction of the greatest slopes; they will collect the rain-water and prevent the ground occupied from becoming wet.

Kitchens, washing-places, corrals, and native camps will be placed to windward of the camp for Europeans. Filth, *débris* of the kitchen or abattoirs, litter, etc., will be incinerated daily.

It is impracticable in the temporary camps to use the movable *tinettes* so happily employed in cantonments in Tong-King, Dahomey, and Madagascar, to prevent infection and the contamination of drinking-water. Arbors and screens will then be erected in conformity with the ministerial decision of August 22, 1889. The precautions there enjoined are the more important because in a march to the front all the troops will be succeeded upon the same ground.

A failure to observe the dispositions so wisely prescribed would risk infecting the camping-places, especially if they are occupied for any considerable length of time.

Whenever the encampment is to be of some duration, all the effects and bedding will be taken out and aired. In the absence of a camp bed, one can be made upon the ground by the aid of straw or herbs covered with the water-proof.

The sick will always be installed in the most favorable places and sent to the rear as soon as possible by the means provided for that purpose and according to the rules adopted.

HYGIENIC PRESCRIPTIONS.

Everything which increases strength of resistance, including excellent quarters, good food, well-adapted clothing and equipment, abstention from all exaggerated fatigue and from all overwork, constitute, and always will constitute, the best protection for troops in campaign.

There are, however, other means to employ in order to prevent certain endemic and epidemic diseases.

Hygiene prevents paludism, but it is not a useless measure to have recourse to therapeutics also, and the moment seems to have arrived for saying a word about the quinine preventive.

There would be temerity in affirming that quinine employed preventively annihilates absolutely the effects of malaria; but it seems certain that it greatly diminishes the severity of serious forms and that it makes the prognosis of the disease less difficult. In a general way, it considerably lessens the effects of paludism. Its value as a preventive rests to-day on a number of facts sufficiently great and positive. No testimony seriously attributes to it a danger or real inconvenience. In fact, it has never been observed that men attacked by fever in spite of the quinine administered preventively have ever become refractory to the medicine when the explicit signs appeared.

The results of experience in the preventive administration of quinine may be thus summarized: 1. Diminution in the number of accesses, which reappear only on the seventh, fourteenth, and twenty-first days. 2. Mildness of the attacks affecting a regular type. 3. Rareness of pernicious attacks, of bilious forms, and of cachexy.

Before going out in the morning in a marshy country, a cup of black coffee and a dose of quinine should be taken if a day of extraordinary fatigue or considerable exposure to the sun is foreseen. In order that the preventive quinine may have a really efficacious action, it should be taken in a dose of at least .3 of a gram, and in certain cases it should be increased to .5 of a gram and even .75 of a gram.

The diminution in the effects of paludism is appreciable only when the sulphate of quinine is administered, not in daily, almost homeopathic and insufficient doses, but in relatively large doses, twice a week or when special circumstances require.

During the Madagascar expedition of 1895, quinine was distributed to the men in doses of from .1 to .2 of a gram during the first four days of the week. In spite of this measure, the fever attacked our soldiers cruelly. It must not be concluded from this, however, that the quinine preventive is useless; it can only be said that the doses were insufficient, or, rather, that the poisoning was too violent.

Alcoholism is the more formidable because it acts upon the organs weakened by heat and impedes digestion, thus aggravating certain diseases, such as paludism and dysentery. The rum of the ration ought to be suppressed and replaced by tea, which would also make it necessary to boil the water. The English have profited on several expeditions by the suppression of rum. The dangers of absinthe and of adulterated liquors are too well known and to fatal in war not to justify the most rigorous severity against the dealers.

The prevention of venereal diseases, which are one of the plagues of the native populations, ought to be an object of constant attention. It would be useful to establish a dispensary. Venereal diseases should not excuse men from work or from taking part in operations unless they are of exceptional gravity. The patients kept in the cantonment should be narrowly watched to prevent a propagation of the disease.

Every precaution should be taken in regard to variola. The health service will be provided with a quantity of vaccine sufficient to revaccinate all the men. They will be revaccinated at the time of embarking or during the course of the voyage. The operation should take place in time to allow the pustules to cicatrize before the disembarkation.

To prevent the importation of cholera or yellow fever, care should be taken to organize a special sanitary police in the region occupied by the troops. Ships will be examined and a lazaret, provided with disinfection apparatus, should receive the sick who are contaminated.

In countries where tetanus is frequent, it will be necessary to carefully disinfect all wounds and to use hypodermic injections with circumspection.

If all the measures we have just enumerated be scrupulously studied and minutely applied, the health of the troops will be greatly profited.

CHAPTER VIII.

Hygienic Principles of a Colonial Army.

To one who sees things as they are, colonial hygiene is in no way opposed to military interests. On the contrary, each page of our books shows how many lives have been saved by the sound application of principles still too often ignored, and how expensive have been the mistakes.

In France, the problem of the organization of a colonial army, so long discussed, seems upon the point of being solved. It is to be feared, however, that the hygienic side will be subordinated to other considerations, and that the new work will be defectively based.

To do it well, new expenses are involved, and the compensation to be realized is not sufficiently remembered. Without speaking of the economy resulting from a limitation of repatriation to strict necessity, and from a diminution in diseases and their consequences—the human capital is well worth something. In a country like ours, where it tends to become more and more rare, it must be husbanded. It should be remembered that nothing is so costly to nations, as to individuals, as *disease*, if it is not *death!*

We establish, as a principle, what may appear a banality, that the colonial army ought to be organized exclusively for the protection and defense of our colonies. The crews of the fleet have not been created to fight on land, but to man the ships. It is essential that this army be constituted with a view to the occupation of our colonial domain, its defense, or its extension. This should be its principal object. However, we presume it would be difficult for the country to understand, if, in a continental war, the only elements of our armies experienced in campaign, and consequently possessing in a high degree the qualities desired to confront the terrible dangers of our future wars, should not be sent to the frontier, where the fate of the nation might be decided, if they were at the time available.

In case of European conflagration we could certainly never have too many troops in the colonies. In view of such an eventuality, our foreign possessions should be strongly garrisoned in times of peace. In case of trouble in Europe, it would be unwise to send troops to the colonies, for, if we are masters of the sea, our colonies will have little to fear from enterprises of the enemy; in the contrary case, all reinforcements sent would be seriously compromised. The greater part of these *élite* troops should therefore be immediately utilized at the frontier.

The colonial army, having a special end, should have a special organization, and the soldier, who is the principal part of the machine, ought to be specialized; his career should be that of a specialist, and he should be a picked man in the full meaning of the word.

Everything in our institutions of to-day is opposed to this view and tends to bend new creations to the common level. Thus from a sentiment as human as it is patriotic, a single gun-shot cannot now be heard without an immediate declaration on the part of every soldier that he is ready for action; each one wishes to take part in the struggle, to confront the dangers, and to derive the advantages. Where glory is to be conquered, there is some for all!

The error of all this is manifest; in a time of progress and of extreme specialization, the professional workman must be always true to his specialty, and the chosen apparatus adapted to the effect to be produced. *To everyone his trade.*

Now, we affirm that nothing in European warfare, or in

its preparation, fits the continental army for tropical expeditions; moreover, the military life and operations of our troops in Algiers bear small resemblance to what these ought to be in the colonies.

The glorious part played by the troops of the Marine at Bazeilles, in the armies of the North and East, proves, on the other hand, that the soldier who has campaigned in the colonies is adapted to make war upon all battle-fields. The reciprocal is not true. So, we believe it is right to demand an autonomous army, adapted to its special functions, and we maintain that if the constitution of the colonial troops is above all a hygienic creation, its recruitment ought to be absolutely by selection.

This view has been taken by the English, the Dutch, and the Spanish, and it cannot be said, especially of the first, that they have not succeeded better than ourselves in the conduct of their expeditions. If the English use their Britannic regiments in their colonies other than India, it is because theirs is an essentially colonial army, by its voluntary enlistment, its organization, its traditions, and the marvelous adaptation of the Anglo-Saxon race to new surroundings.

It is sufficient, moreover, to see with what scrupulous care the English form their European detachments for a foreign expedition, to be convinced that with them the principle, *The right man in the right place*, is the chief concern.

The flag of France has always been gloriously defended; but the sacrifices have often greatly surpassed the limits of necessity; sometimes they have even been disproportioned to the end in view and the results obtained.

It is therefore necessary to determine what should be done to diminish the bloody tithe paid by France for the protection and extension of the colonial domain, and what economic measures will compensate for the new expenses imposed by the rational organization of a veritable colonial army.

§ I. *Recruiting.*

We have seen what enemies the colonial soldier has to combat, the extraordinary fatigues which sometimes have to be endured, and how necessary it is, in spite of all the precautions taken to protect him, that he should possess the maximum degree of physical resistance, for at certain times he will have no other safeguard.

Age.—The first condition to exact from the colonial soldier is sufficient age. If too young, he is a ready prey to all tropical diseases. Experience shows that an insufficient bodily development unfits him to bear the fatigues of an expedition. If he is robust, he will resist, perhaps, for several years, but will end by succumbing before he is 30.

In England, a soldier must be 21 years old and have a year of service before being sent to the colonies; he must be 22 before he is allowed to form part of a column there.

In France, we have had soldiers of 19 and even of 18 years of age in the colonies in recent years; many of them have never again seen their native land! Should 21 or 22 years be accepted as the limit? We answer formally: Neither the one nor the other, unless great difficulty should be encountered in recruiting with a higher age limit. Indeed, in our opinion, soldiers younger than 23 should not be sent to the colonies. It is only at that age that there is a certainty of complete development.

M. Morache goes farther in fixing the inferior age limit for the colonies at 25. According to him, the maximum of resistance to fatigue and to morbid causes is found between the ages of 25 and 35.

From what precedes, we consider it necessary to lay down the principle that soldiers of the colonial army should not be sent to the colonies until after they are 22 years old; they could then have finished a certain number of years of service in France or in Algeria. They would thus be doubly tempered by age and by military service. High pay and retirement after fifteen years' service, with proportionate advantages for those whose health would permit a service of only a third or two-thirds of that period, would be sufficient to attract and retain the soldiers.

We would thus imitate the English in the Indies, the Spaniards in the Philippines, and the Dutch in their Asiatic possessions.

Up to 32 years of age, the enlistment would permit every soldier to have finished at least one period of service in France, all being calculated so that the retirements could be made before the age of 45.

Nevertheless, a soldier who is 40 years old and has not attained a non-commissioned grade should be placed in proportional retirement, whatever be his time of colonial service. One grows old quickly in the colonies; soldiers over 40 should not be in the ranks; even that age is an extreme limit. The most favorable period will always be from 23 to 35 years, and it should be surpassed only in exceptional cases. The *old soldier* is not, and never has been, what he has been considered. The *grognards* of Austerlitz and of Waterloo were volunteers of the wars of the Revolution and many of the soldiers of the Old Guard had not passed 30 years! If they were old, it was not by reason of age, but because they had lived much war; they had seen so much of it!

In the colonies, even more than in Europe, the inconveniences of an age too advanced are the same as those of an age too young. *Old soldiers*, as we understand the term, are excellent, but *soldiers too old in years* are worthless.

Condition of Health.—Is it necessary to say that every colonial soldier should possess not only the physical qualifications necessary to the soldier of the metropolitan army, but should also be in excellent health?

A medical commission, and not one surgeon alone, should examine the men to be enlisted or reënlisted, and it should be the same for the non-commissioned officers. Outside of the ports, this commission could meet at the chief place in each department.

The medical leaf of the soldier's hand-book, containing everything of importance connected with his health during his first term of service in the active army, would then be of the greatest aid. The health service as well as the administration would derive great advantage from consulting it.

Those enlisted and reënlisted should be exempt from every constitutional defect; they should be affected neither with consumption, nor rheumatism, nor alcoholism, nor be convalescents from any serious malady whatever.

We have seen why a predisposition to tuberculosis should be inquired into; in spite of Bondin's theory, that disease is a sure auxiliary of paludism and *vice versa*.

Dyspeptics, the obese, those with rheumatism and cardialgia should be eliminated. They are future good-for-nothings.

It is known how quickly the digestive functions are influenced by a heat of long duration. The liver and the stomach, then, should be in excellent condition. Even a light attack of these organs is weakening. The repair of the tissues is slower, the destruction of the organic poisons is more difficult, especially if the liver, "that great chemist of the system," as Ch. Richet has said, is no longer the seat of excrementitial activity. The deplorable tendency of those having rheumatism to become cold is also known, and we have seen that one grows cold in the Tropics quicker than anywhere else, because there is always an increased propensity to uncover on account of the heat. In these conditions, a light breeze rising after a stifling calm causes a brusque modification of the hygrometric condition of the air sufficiently great to produce great variations in the evaporation from the skin. It is during the winter that these transitions are most frequent, and it is for this reason that the winter season is so unfavorable to those who have rheumatism.

It is also necessary to mistrust men subject to local hyperhidrosis, slight but frequent muscular pains, headaches, nose-bleed, fluent hemorrhoids, abundant deposits of urates in the urine, habitual eczematous eruptions—in a word, to the little things making up the small change of arthritis.

Cardiac hypertrophies, whatever the cause, even from growth and independent of all valvular lesion, should be regarded as disqualifying for colonial service. Experience teaches that men thus affected, as well as those addicted to the use of alcohol, are the first victims of sun-stroke.

Observation has shown that one does not become acclimated to fever any more than to dysentery or hepatitis; that, on the contrary, one becomes the more subject to these affections the more the system has been prepared by former attacks, for no "vaccination" is known which creates immunity from them. That is to say, every confirmed victim of paludism, every former sufferer from dysentery, every man having an enlarged liver or spleen, should find no place in the colonial contingents.

By making it possible for the officers and surgeons to look for and ascertain organic defects or the presence of morbid germs, and by obliging the soldier to serve at least two years before admitting him to the first reënlistment, it would, be possible to obtain that recruitment by selection which is indispensable in the organization of a good colonial army. Then the anomalies so frequent under the system now in vogue would be seen no longer. Young volunteers enlisted for five years are now permitted to reënlist for another five years, and are thus found, at the age of $18\frac{1}{2}$, bound to the service for more than *nine years*. It is still more regrettable that young men of this category, with more than eight years to serve, should be invalided for affections the germs of which existed at the time of their enlistment and which have developed in the first years of service.*

Moral Conditions.—To the conditions of physical vigor represented by suitable age and good health, are joined others of a different nature, but also indispensable. *Mens sana in corpore sano*, in the broadest sense, could never be better applied than here to depict the union of the physical and moral qualities which should be possessed by the future colonial soldier.

Every man serving in the colonies should be a *volunteer*, a man enlisted or reënlisted of his own free will, and on that account naturally well paid. That is what makes the strength of the English and Dutch colonial armies.

Voluntary enlistment and sufficient age give the men of the Foreign Legion that strength of resistance, that ardor, which makes them such marvelous soldiers, especially in campaign. "The Legion," says M. de Villebois-Mareuil, "has a double character: men are enlisted up to the age of 40; it is composed of soldiers by trade, to whom the career of arms

---

*By a decision dated the 15th of May, 1897, the Minister of Marine has fortunately applied a restrictive measure to the provisions of the decree of the 4th of August, 1894, which authorized such a state of things; under this decision, the first reënlistment is limited to three years. This makes it possible for a man, six months after his enlistment, to bind himself to service for only seven and a half in place of nine and a half years.

is a refuge, the daily bread, often a title of naturalization—that is to say, for a time at least, a veritable profession. In this hybrid organization, which a man enters masked, without paper of identity or of nationality, without extract from judicial pigeon-holes, without anything which recommends him or which speaks of his past—there is a strange mixture; but it may be said that from this indefinable whole is evolved an energy of iron, an instinctive passion for adventure, an astonishing fertility of initiative, a supreme disdain for death, all the sublime originalities of martial virtues."

In spite of this fine portrait, which is a very good one of the *legionaire*, we do not believe it represents the prototype of the colonial soldier.

Some soldiers of the Legion are too old, others too difficult to manage. Sublime under fire, stoical in the presence of danger, endowed with an enormous resistance to fatigue, they are the first soldiers of the world for a strong blow or for an expedition of short duration; but their chiefs know how hard it is for them to bear garrison life and the monotony of daily service, and how much discipline costs them, for they possess to a high degree the faults of their generous qualities; love of the unknown, of the new, often leads these men into strange adventures, especially as nothing except the battle-field attaches them to the flag they serve so heroically; and the administration which has at its disposal, in a distant colony, only such elements as this, in face of the natives, might one day find itself in a situation as annoying as critical.

In the colonies, more than in Europe, men of *good conduct*, upon whom the chief can always count, are needed in the ranks. Now, it is impossible to trust, in ordinary times, men who see in colonial life only the means of escaping the exigencies of European discipline. Inclined to violate all orders, hygienic rules will not stop them, and their indocility will often expose them, as well as their commanders, to the most cruel disappointments.

Men of bad character during their sojourn in France, especially drunkards, ought to be rigorously discarded. In a hot country, the habits of a well-regulated life, of sobriety, are indispensable to the maintenance of discipline.

Thus, in certain circumstances, the *disciplinaires* have rendered service under fire; but they have a resistance much inferior to that of the other white troops. We have seen that in Senegal, where their mortality was triple that of the other troops. It is true they have been employed in certain colonies on the construction and maintenance of roads; it may doubtless be said, also, that they occupy unhealthy posts in place of free soldiers. Where is the advantage? Have we not natives for the last service? If the *disciplinaires* lost three times as many men as the other European corps in Senegal, they had a proportionate number of sick; they are then very expensive, and it is difficult to understand why the State thus maintains in service, at great expense, troops which are worth less than either the *infanterie de marine* or the natives under fire, and are very far from the worth of these in the ordinary conditions of colonial life.

The place of these men excluded from the Army ought to be in the military workshops of France, Algeria, and the colonies, and not in the ranks of the armed contingents. In the campaign in Upper Senegal, in 1886 and 1887, the mortality among the *disciplinaires* was very great.

As for recruiting the colonial soldiers among the vagabonds, the habitual criminals, it is to be seen from what precedes how little that is to be thought of. Here to morally defective qualities is joined a physical debility the more accentuated in the case of these individuals by life in the prisons where they have usually been confined. Anyone who has seen a convoy of criminals in New Caledonia knows that among these worn-out men there is no longer either activity or energy. The climate would quickly overcome these miserable creatures, who are fitter subjects for the asylum than for the prison or the barracks.

We insist, with Doctor Maurel, upon the necessity of having in the colonial army, from top to bottom, a recruitment by selection in regard to moral and intellectual qualities. The functions of initiative and responsibility of the officers and non-commissioned officers should not be ignored. As to the soldiers, their attitude towards the natives should be a worthy one and their conduct should be irreproachable. They are not sent to the colonies to endanger our influence, but, on the contrary, to contribute to its extension.

Conditions of Race.—It has been thought that men of the warm countries of the south of Europe were more apt to support the intertropical climates, as tropical anæmia has long been considered a *thermic* anæmia. Certain facts seem to justify this hypothesis. Abscess of the liver is twice as common among the French of the North as among those of the South. Thévenot has observed that yellow fever attacks men of the North in the proportion of five to one of the South.

Is it true that the appearance of tropical anæmia is slower among the Southerners? It would be better, like Navarre, to attribute their greater endurance, their faculty of resistance to disease, to their habitual sobriety; when drinkers, the Southerners resist hot climates no better than the others.

In another manner, an idea may be formed of the influence of alcoholism upon the proportional mortality of men of different regions of France, of different manners and habits, while submitted to the same kind of life and the same work.

Some interesting observations may be made by considering the mortality among those entering the Navy from the French littoral, from 1891 to 1895:

Algeria and Corsica............Mortality   2.20 per 1000
Mediterranean littoral..........Mortality   6.52 per 1000
Paris and the North littoral....Mortality   7.10 per 1000
Region of the Normandy coasts...Mortality   9.30 per 1000
Region of the Southwest.........Mortality 10.40 per 1000
Brittany........................Mortality 13.20 per 1000

The difference between the Corsicans and Provençals, on the one hand, and the Bretons, on the other, is striking.

The habits of men have an influence on mortality much more than the place they come from. It would also be better to take into account the *temperament* of the individual than his place of origin. According to Corre, the major part of the European elements of the colonial army should be recruited among the dark-complexioned; a fair man now and then presents a fine appearance of physical vigor, but to support the fatigues of the service his system needs a too heavy ration of meat. It is to be observed, moreover, that the English in India are more often attacked by hepatitis in all degrees than the Spaniards in Cuba and the Antilles.

In the question which now occupies us, that of *race* is one of the most important of all the conditions.

Is the acclimatization of the European in the intertropical countries possible? In any case it is not easy and requires great effort. *In tropical countries, the European can live only in a weakened state.* Lind says: "The men may be likened to vegetables transplanted in foreign soil, where they can be preserved and acclimated only by extraordinary care."

Acclimatization is the ordeal to which the system is subjected and with which it pays the expenses of becoming accustomed to the hot country. All the new climatic conditions of the tropical countries, to which must often be joined a defective condition of the soil and of the localities inhabited, tend to modify the physiological functions of the new arrival. A man who is careful supports the meteorological change easily enough; the telluric influences alone are a formidable danger.

This practically coincides with what Felix Jacquot and Dutrouleau have said: "In the various countries, two conditions are encountered: the first, irremovable, resulting from the climatological surroundings; the other, accidental and more or less removable; for example, paludal conditions. The European is acclimated to the first, becoming like the natives, who bear them more or less easily; it is only with great difficulty that he is acclimated to the second." Newcomers, whether Europeans or natives, pay their tribute to the poison of the marsh, with the difference that the first, debilitated by the climate, are more accessible to every morbific cause.

The Caucasian race has succeeded in acclimating itself in many of the countries of the torrid zone. Where it has not been able to implant itself, the obstacle has been the endemic diseases born of the soil. It cannot be said that the French are not acclimated in the Antilles. The emancipation of the blacks, by diminishing the fortunes, has done more than to retard European immigration, a number of families having abandoned the colony and returned to France.

It has been seen how the Spaniards have acclimated themselves in Cuba and in the Greater Antilles, where the climatic conditions are the same as in the French and English Antilles. The births there are more numerous than the deaths; fecundity is greater than in Europe. Acclimatization is made by selection—that is, by the elimination of all those unsuited to the climate. Is not that a proof that the European is capable of being acclimatized there?

It would be wrong to claim that no acclimatization or naturalization is possible unless the emigrant can work the soil with impunity. This objection is answered, on the one hand, by the agricultural colonies of Brazil, and on the other, by the fact that it is not necessary to go to the Tropics in order to suffer from the emanations from freshly removed soil; fever caused by clearing the ground is common to all countries; it is only more severe in tropical countries, and we have seen that it also attacks the natives.

Blacks and Europeans are equally sensible to dysentery and hepatitis and never become immune to them.

Both pay their tribute to yellow fever; a former attack, however, renders the individual immune; and a series of attacks gives immunity to a race, for a time at least, as is the case with the negros of Senegal and Sierra-Leone. If the Houssa blacks were transported to Senegambia at the time of an epidemic, they would no doubt be attacked, because they are not immune to yellow fever. This has only too often been the case when the coolies of India have been transported to Guiana.

It is seen that the white race is not more disfavored than the Asiatic and African races in regard to tropical endemo-epidemics. It would even seem that the European is the most cosmopolitan of men; but that does not mean that he can be transported with impunity to no matter what part of the world. There are unhealthy countries which should be interdicted to him until they are rendered healthy, and for this purpose native manual-labor—above all, local manual labor—should always be reserved.

Nevertheless, it is not rare to find intertropical countries where the European can live several years without danger, by the aid of a wise hygiene, and where the colonial army may become a nursery of colonists. For that purpose, it would be sufficient to ameliorate the condition of the non-commissioned officers and soldiers, to treat them as the English and Dutch treat their colonial soldiers, in the Indies and in Java, by permitting marriage and by giving a renewable leave, after a certain length of service, to those of excellent conduct who would undertake to settle in the colony in which they were serving.*

§ II. *Organization.*

It is not rare to hear it said that it is useless to create a colonial army; that it is sufficient to organize it, inasmuch as that army already exists. It is also said that it would be for the best if, conformably to the military laws, the Marine should organize, command, administer, care for, and pay its troops wherever they may be found, in France, in the colonies, and in foreign countries. From an administrative standpoint this is perfectly correct; from a hygiene standpoint it is not sufficient.

As long as nothing is done to recruit the constituent elements of that organization; as long as it is impossible to judiciously select the men to form the colonial army; as long as soldiers sent to the colonies are limited to those who are too young or too weak—France will possess regiments beyond the seas, but she will not have the instrument indispensable to the economic expansion of her colonial power.

---

*It has been thought that our Senegalese and Houssa tirailleurs, who have been, as is known, an excellent instrument in the conquest of Madagascar, might advantageously become an instrument of colonization not less valuable. The Chinese and Annamites make excellent colonists wherever they go. We think it would be well, in the interest of colonization, to favor this kind of expansion, in order to show the way to the European colonists.

We have established the conditions to be fulfilled to make a good colonial soldier:
1. To be a volunteer.
2. To be in excellent health and old enough.
3. To have performed two years of obligatory military service in France.
4. To be of good character.

It is with such elements that we are going to consider the organization of the special forces necessary to the occupation of our colonies and to the formation of expeditionary corps.

The principle is to place a *European head* on a *native body*.

Colonial Corps.—In making a comparative study between foreign troops employed in the colonies and the French colonial troops, it seems to us, at first, that our country is behind what is done abroad. But, in order to be rational, the calculation ought to be made for each of our colonies in comparison with a foreign colony of the same class. It would be possible to compare, for example, the effectives of Algeria with those of India; those of Reunion with those of Mauritius or of Aden; those of Sierra-Leone with those of Senegal.

Under these restrictions, we can make some comparisons, but they will have only a relative value. Thus, when speaking of the effectives maintained by the English in the colonies, it is forgotten that they have 2000 to 3000 men at Aden, and as many at Mauritius; that they have very strong garrisons at Hong-Kong, Singapore, etc.

The effectives of the English army in India, without counting the troops of the rajahs, are in the proportion of 1 European to 3 natives. In Burmah, there is only 1 Englishman to 4 foreigners. The recruitment of the English army of India, in so far as the native elements are concerned, is by voluntary enlistment. The contract stipulates that those enlisted may be employed in all parts of the Indian Empire and even outside.

Holland maintains 30,000 men in the East Indies, of whom 14,000 are Europeans and 16,000 natives, or 46 per cent of the one and 54 of the other.

In the Philippines, Spain maintains 12,000 men, mostly Malays with European officers.

With us the troops that make up the colonial service are thus constituted:

    13 regiments of *infanterie de marine;*
    2 regiments of *artillerie de marine;*
    5 companies of mechanics;
    1 corps of *disciplinaires;*
    1 company of *fusiliers de discipline;*
    10 native regiments.

To these must be added detachments of engineers and of cavalry, several battalions of the Foreign Legion furnished by the Department of War, and a corps of colonial *gendarmes*, formed of elements detached from the companies in France.

Distribution of Effectives.—The troops of the Marine intended for colonial service comprise Europeans and natives. We are especially interested to know the relative proportion of each of these groups.*

The European troops serve in France and in the colonies.

In France, there are 8 regiments of *infanterie de marine*, 2 regiments of *artillerie de marine*, and some companies of artificers and mechanics. The strength is about 16,000 men, the *infanterie de marine* numbering 12,000.

---

*Economy must not be neglected when the question is considered of increasing the number of native soldiers, in order to proportionally diminish the number of European soldiers. The calculations of M. Fleury-Ravarin show that a European soldier costs from 2127 to 2540 fr.; a Soudanese tirailleur costs only 1189 fr.; a Senegalese, 980 fr.; a native of Tong-King, 550 fr.

These regiments constitute the *dépôts* and provide for the recruitment and relief of the colonial corps. Constant changes are made between them and the colonial garrisons.

In the colonies, the European troops are variously distributed.

The *infanterie de marine* has in Tong-King and Annam, the 9th and 10th regiments, each of 12 companies; in Cochin-China, 8 companies of the 11th regiment; in New Caledonia, 6 companies of the 12th regiment; in Madagascar, the 13th regiment of 12 companies; in Senegal, a battalion of 4 companies; in Reunion, a battalion of 4 companies, 2 of which are detached to Madagascar; in Guiana, a battalion of 4 companies; in Martinique, a battalion of 3 companies; in Guadeloupe, a detachment; in Tahiti, a detachment; in all, about 9000 Europeans.

The artillery and the companies of artillery mechanics are distributed in the colonies in two groups: the first in Cochin-China and Oceania, the second in Africa and the Antilles.

The first group furnishes: in Tong-King and Annam, 1 *direction*, 6 batteries, some companies of mechanics, and some guides and pontoniers; in Cochin-China, 1 *direction*, 2 batteries, and some mechanics; in New Caledonia, 1 *direction*, 1 battery, and some mechanics; in Tahiti, a detachment and some mechanics; about 1400 Europeans.

The second group furnishes: in Senegal, 1 *direction*, 2 batteries, some mechanics and guides; in the Soudan, 1 *direction*, 1 battery, and some mechanics; in Martinique, 1 *direction*, 1 battery, and some mechanics; in Guadeloupe, 1 detachment; in Guiana, 1 *direction* and 1 detachment; in Madagascar, 1 *direction*, 3 batteries, and some mechanics; in Reunion, 1 *direction*, 1 detachment, and some mechanics; about 1100 Europeans.

There are besides a corps of *disciplinaires* and a company of *fusiliers de discipline* with a common *dépôt* at the island of Oleron. The corps of *disciplinaires* furnishes detachments to Senegal and Madagascar; the company of *fusiliers de discipline* sends a detachment to Martinique: in all, 599 Europeans.

It is also necessary to include 1500 Europeans constituting the *cadres* of the native regiments. We thus arrive at an approximate total of 14,000 Europeans in service in the colonies and belonging to the *infanterie* and *artillerie de marine* and to the *disciplinaires*.

The European element is also represented by the troops of the Foreign Legion, companies of engineers, detachments of cavalry and *gendarmes*, making about 2000 men. Adding the troops loaned by the Department of War to the number of troops of the Marine, a total of 16,000 men is reached.

There are 10 regiments of native troops: 1 regiment of Senegalese tirailleurs of 12 companies; 1 regiment of Soudanese tirailleurs of 16 companies; 1 regiment of Annamite tirailleurs of 12 companies; 2 regiments of Tong-King tirailleurs of 12 companies; 2 regiments of Tong-King tirailleurs of 16 companies; 1 colonial mixed regiment, in Madagascar, formed of Houssas and Senegalese, of 12 companies; 2 regiments of Malagasy tirailleurs of 12 companies; in all, 23,000 natives.

It is well to note that there are native troops in only three of our colonies: in Senegal and the Soudan, Indo-China, and Madagascar. It may be said, however, that the proportion of the European element is still too great and that it ought to be reduced.

Formation of the Contingents.—To obtain this result the preparatory scheme would be:

1. To organize new native units.

2. To use all the colonial contingents furnished by the local recruitment.

3. To send only such European troops as are strictly necessary.

To classify these ideas, the service of *occupation* must be distinguished from that of *expedition*.

1. Service of Occupation.

The troops of occupation are those charged with the security of the colony and forming the nucleus of the forces intended to provide for its defense in case of war.

It was recently suggested to take the company of *infanterie de marine* from Guadeloupe, and M. Gerville-Réache rightly opposed the project. As in Algeria, it is necessary to have in our old colonies the nuclei of European troops to suppress troubles before which the *gendarmerie* and local police would be found impotent. The last anti-Semitic movement in Algeria might be cited in support of this theory. In the end too great a reduction on the score of economy might be bitterly regretted.

However, the service of occupation ought to be assured, in greater part, by the local troops of the country itself, well supplied with European officers, but supported:

1. By European artillery;
2. By *gendarmes* in sufficient number;
3. By bodies of European infantry in countries not yet fully pacified.

In Tong-King, the Soudan, and Madagascar, European troops will be needed for a long time yet and in sufficient number to conduct a campaign, with others in reserve, to guard against eventualities. In the Antilles, Reunion, New Caledonia, Cochin-China, and Senegal a few units of European artillery and infantry are alone necessary.

In the pacified colonies the *gendarmes* ought, indeed, to constitute the principal force to guarantee security in ordinary times. There is already a company of *gendarmerie* in Guadeloupe, Martinique, Guiana, Reunion, and New Caledonia, and a detachment in Tahiti. The *gendarmes* are excellent colonial soldiers; they live *en famille* and take care of their health; it is a type upon which to model our sendentary soldiers.

2. *Expeditions beyond the Sea and Dépôts.*

To provide this service and at the same time to furnish the reliefs and constitute the necessary *cadres* for the numerous native units, there must be a solid reserve in France, which, with the elements present in the colonies, shall constitute the colonial army.

We have seen with what elements we would wish to constitute it; a word now about its organization proper.

In France there are as many *gendarmes* as are wanted; it would probably be possible to have as many Frenchmen as could be desired in the colonial army by offering sufficient advantages to attract men from 22 to 32 years of age, desirous of enlisting for five years with the privilege of reënlisting two or three times, according to age; by offering all who have a taste for a life of adventure an honorable career and sufficient pay to prevent a hesitation on their part to embracing it.

In this manner the country would have a body of *élite* and the means of developing colonization.

The system to employ is that of high pay, increasing with each reënlistment, retirement after fifteen years' service, and concessions of land and employment for those who wish to remain in the colonies.

The system of bounties for enlistment and reënlistment should be suppressed as soon as possible. It is wrong. It would be more logical to base the pecuniary advantages upon an increase of pay, or, better still, to reserve the bounties for the time when the men leave the Army.

The bounty, as now given, is a source of abuse and debauchery, prejudicial to health and discipline. Many soldiers spend it within a few days; sometimes it is even spent before being received, because shameless speculators advance the money with usury.

The present troops of the Marine, better recruited, increased, profiting by the laws, decrees, and regulations which govern the land forces, especially the advantages created by the law of the *cadres*, provided with all the accessory services,* could constitute the base of an autonomous *colonial army*, divided into two parts.

MOBILE ORGANIZATIONS OF COLONIAL INFANTRY AND ARTILLERY.

Their *rôle* should be to furnish the colonial garrisons with officers and soldiers; in case of an expedition, they should be ready to go, as a whole or by fractions, to the colonies. Should there be a continental war, they would constitute an army corps to coöperate on the frontier with troops of the land army. Their units should be kept complete; the officers, non-commissioned officers, and men who compose them should all be ready to take the field.

They should consist of two divisions of infantry, a brigade of artillery, and a battalion of colonial engineers.

DISTRICT ORGANIZATION.

Their *rôle* should be to receive the officers, non-commissioned officers, and soldiers in excess in the mobile organi-

---

*The colonial army would necessarily have an administrative service and a health service, which should be under control of its commander. The abuses resulting from the separation of the powers have been pointed out by M. Cabart-Danneville.

zations, and especially all sent back from the colonies, as long as their state of health requires. These district organizations should also constitute large *dépôts* for the mobile organizations; they might be charged with the instruction of the volunteer recruits.

There could be taken from these organizations the units maintained at Paris and those which the Government might consider it necessary to maintain at other points—at Lyons, for example—not only in time of peace, but even during the first days of mobilization, until the arrival of the contingents of the territorial army.

The district organizations should be stationed in proximity to the positions they would occupy at the time of mobilization, and, in case of continental war, they would have the mission of assuring, from the first hour, the defense of the military ports and of their zones of action; they could continue to be used for that defense and to serve as *dépôts* for mobile organizations. Finally, if the nature of the war required, they could furnish the elements of a second army corps for use on the frontier.

In the beginning, the mobile organizations would receive the reserves of the colonial army; the district organizations would receive a part of these reserves and those from the naval lists not utilized by the Marine, who might be turned over to them in time of peace.

Two new divisions of infantry, a brigade of artillery, and a battalion of colonial engineers would be indispensable for these district organizations.

The expense of maintaining such a colonial army in France in time of peace, it is true, would be considerable if that army comprised only those enlisted for from four to five years and the reënlisted; but it must be remembered that each regiment of *infanterie* and *artillerie de marine* includes about one-fifth of its strength as company artisans or mechanics without rank—musicians, clerks, orderlies, employees of various kinds, etc. By reason of the nature of their service, most of these men should be kept in France for several consecutive years, and should, therefore, be exempt during this time from colonial service. It would be the same for the mobile and district organizations of the colonial army.

It would thus be indispensable, in order to make all who reënlist available for colonial service, to make voluntary enlistments of three years to occupy these places. Those enlisted in this manner will furnish material for the organization of the colonial army and excellent men for reënlistment at the expiration of their term of service. They will take the field with their organizations, in a continental war, etc., but they should not be sent to the colonies until they have reached the age of 22. The principle that only fully developed men should be sent to the colonies will not be violated by the adoption of this mode of recruiting, which can work concurrently with that of voluntary enlistments for four and five years.

Before enumerating the advantages of the system proposed, it is proper to recall the changes which have taken place in the *infanterie de marine*.

Different Organizations of the Infanterie de Marine.—At its origin, the *infanterie de marine*, instituted by decree of the 14th of May, 1831, comprised two regiments having 58 companies in the colonies and 6 *dépôt* companies in France, with an effective total of 233 officers and 4966 men.

Successively reorganized by the ordinances of the 20th of November, 1838, the 7th of November, 1843, and the 21st of March, 1847; the order of the 24th of August, 1848; the decree of the 31st of August, 1854; the imperial decision of the 8th of January, 1859; the decrees of the 26th of November,

1869, the 26th of January, 1880, and the 1st of March, 1890; this corps to-day includes more than 1600 officers, 25,000 European troops, and 23,000 native troops. The European troops comprise 185 companies of *infanterie de marine*, of which 65 are in the colonies. The native troops comprise 182 companies.

These various acts of organization, which do not include those relating to the native corps, may be divided into two groups: the first, from 1831 to 1854; the second, from 1854 to 1897. The principle of organization is different for each of these periods.

In the first period it was possible to supply, well or badly, the colonial relief. The conditions of recruitment were very different from those of to-day, notably since 1868; non-commissioned officers and soldiers were almost exclusively volunteer recruits or substitutes—that is to say, recruits easy to instruct, or old soldiers, placed in organizations whose non-commissioned officers had repeatedly served in the colonies.

With a *personnel* thus composed and contingents available for colonial service, it was possible, almost immediately after the call of a class, to have at the *dépôt* the same number of companies as in the colonies. When it was impossible to relieve them, men were left in the colonies five or six years, as was the case in the La Plata expedition, the war of the Crimea, and the expedition to Mexico. The non-commissioned officers and privates passed seven years with the colors; many reënlisted or served as substitutes in the corps in the colonies themselves.

The period of colonial service was four years; it was thus only necessary to relieve a quarter of the garrisons beyond the sea each year; those who returned to France on account of disease were fewer in a *personnel* composed of fully developed men and old soldiers. Moreover, the large effective strength in each colony allowed great latitude; vacancies were filled only once a year, at the time of the relief of the companies, which took place in the most favorable season according to colony, and in accordance with the wise provisions of the royal ordinance of the 25th of January, 1828. The causes for changes were much less than they are to-day.

In the second period, regiments replaced the *dépôts* in the ports and constituted the central portions; moreover, the advantage of having only light troops in the Marine being definitely recognized, the regiments received the armament of the *chasseurs à pied*.

In reality, the decree of the 31st of August, 1854, organized the Marine as it existed up to 1890. But the proportion of 70 companies in France to 50 in the colonies, which was sufficient at the time the decree was promulgated to insure the regular relief of the companies and the maintenance of the effectives beyond the sea, was so no longer when it became necessary to organize, with the resources of the central portions, expeditionary battalions for the Crimea, Greece, Indo-China, etc. It thus happened that in 1857 there were companies in the Antilles which had left France six years before.

The need of large detachments in the Extrême-Orient becoming felt more and more, it was necessary to seek the resources which the metropolis could not furnish in the garrisons of the colonies where order seemed definitely established.

In 1859, with a view to remedying this troublesome state of affairs, the number of companies in France was increased and the number of companies in the colonies was reduced; the strength was 12,613 men, of whom 8578 were in France, and 4035 in the colonies. The expeditionary companies were taken from France; and if one goes back to all that has been done with this reduced effective strength, and compares it with what is done at the present time, one is again impressed with this truth: "Only seasoned troops can resist colonial climates; recruits melt like snow."

In the first years which followed the reörganization of 1859, the conditions of colonial service were very good: the men sent from France were instructed and fully developed, the organizations were solid.

The decree of the 26th of November, 1869, had the object, while assuring the regular working of the central portions with reference to the requirements of our new colonial garrisons, of harmonizing the organization of the army with the new condition of the law of 1868, which reduced to five years the time the men of the different classes were to pass with the colors. The *infanterie de marine* was composed of 140 companies, with a total effective of 16,646 men—8703 in France, and 7943 in the colonies.

Thus there was maintained nearly one man in France to one in the colonies.

This proportion was far from being sufficient. By reason of losses of all kinds and sick-leaves from the *dépôts*, there was a continual deficiency of men, at the ports, available for colonial service. Thus the origin of all the difficulties of the *infanterie de marine* in providing the colonial relief is to be ascribed to the organization of 1869.

At a given moment, the *infanterie de marine* could not relieve the garrisons outside of Europe in a suitable manner, because of the disproportion between the number of companies maintained in France and the number to be furnished the colonies.

This disproportion was still further increased by the reduction to two years of the time of service in Cochin-China and Senegal, by the strength given to the garrison of New Caledonia, and by the maintenance of a detachment in Tong-King.

The decree of 1880 was the first to admit the principle established by experience, that it was necessary to have in France at least a company and a half in order to maintain one in the colonies. In accordance with that idea, it increased the number of companies of *infanterie de marine* to 176, with 103 in France and 73 in the colonies, and an effective total of 18,758 men: 11,086 in France and 7672 in the colonies.

This proportion, which should never have been disturbed, was not long maintained. The constant increase of the colonial garrisons, without corresponding measures in France, and the creation of a certain number of native corps, the *cadres* of which were furnished by the *infanterie de marine*, rapidly destroyed the proportion laid down by the decree of 1880.

The decree of the 1st of March, 1890, making two regiments from one of the *infanterie de marine*, was especially with the object of applying the fundamental principles of the organization of modern infantry, and the creation of brigades in the ports. At present, the companies maintained in France have an effective of 12,234 men; the colonial garrisons, in the 65 companies and the *cadres* of the numerous native regiments, comprise more than 12,000 European troops.

The situation is precarious, and it is time to apply a remedy, if it is not desired to see those whose principal mission is to guard and defend our colonies, which they moreover helped to conquer, succumb to their troubles.

Advantages of the System Proposed.—It does not seem necessary to insist upon the advantages which would result to the country, and also to the officers, non-commissioned officers, and soldiers, by the adoption of the project we have proposed for the organization of the colonial army.

These advantages may be briefly summarized: the protection or defense of our colonies assured under all circumstances; the protection of our military ports and their approaches, at the time of declaration of war, from an unexpected attack of an audacious enemy; the provision of a valuable support, in case of necessity, to the general defense of the territory, by furnishing two *élite* army corps.

This organization would be of great use if the neighboring continental powers should again mass troops upon our frontiers and we ourselves should be forced to increase our effectives by the restoration of the fourth battalion of the infantry regiments and by the creation of the 20th army corps.

As far as private interests are concerned, the organization of the colonial army in two large subdivisions would have the advantage of furnishing all the officers and non-commissioned officers necessary to the native troops; it would permit every overworked soldier, without change of career, to continue *to serve in his own arm* with his comrades. The advantages would be especially great for the officers, worn out to-day by the colonial service, as shown by the losses they sustain. Moreover, exchanges could be extensively authorized between the elements of the two formations, as they should also be among the officers of the land army and those of the colonial army.

The relief of the officers would be more equitable. The actual situation is truly critical and is aggravated since our taking possession of Madagascar. In 1895, there were 813 officers in France and 650 in the colonies; 1496 non-commissioned officers in France and 1484 in the colonies. At present, we count 775 officers in France, against 1201 in the colonies or in Crete, and 1433 non-commissioned officers in France against 2092 in the colonies or in Crete.

In these conditions, the length of service in France is eighteen months for colonels, twenty-three months for lieutenant-colonels, sixteen for chiefs of battalion, eighteen for captains, eighteen for lieutenants and sub-lieutenants, fifteen for adjutants, eighteen for sergeant-majors, and sixteen for sergeants.

The non-commissioned officers have proportional retirement after fifteen years' service; the officers wait twenty-five years—that is to say, they are worn out by the colonial life at the moment when they should be able to take a well-earned repose. If promotion were regular, there would be less complaint; but it is not; assimilation of rank does not exist in the *infanterie de marine*, as it does in all the other corps in France and in all European armies.

The scheme of M. Cabart-Danneville, which provides 3 officers in France to 2 in the colonies, would be a relief; but the remedy would not be sufficient. The percentage of mortality of the officers, notwithstanding their age and greater comfort, is nearly as great as that of the soldiers. This supports what we have said in regard to tellurism; no person escapes. Tellurism has no respect for rank, and if the officers die as often as their men who go to the colonies too young, it is because they go too often and stay too long in the bad conditions.

To lessen the hardships of the colonial service, it has been proposed to send officers of the land army. That would be a great mistake.

The colonial army ought to suffice for its task, for all its duties. It would not be just to admit the principle that, on the score of economy, officers of the land army could be detached to the colonies, there to occupy places most often privileged, and, after a stay of two or three years, reënter their former corps, benefiting by the rights of promotion or the *Légion d'honneur*, which are only rarely accorded to the officers who consecrate their whole career to this service. It would open the door to favor. As we have said, let exchanges among the officers of the two armies be considerably facilitated—nothing more: the profit will then be for all, and for the country.

Moreover, it is not true that the special competency necessary in the officers who serve in the Tropics is acquired very quickly. It cannot be too strongly insisted, with M. Fleury-Ravarin, that there is a necessity for having in our colonial possessions officers of very special aptitude and education. "We should have a colonial *cadre* strongly enough constituted to have no need of aid from the metropolitan army; the meshes ought to be sufficiently tight to prevent the passage of any and every body." Finally, there ought to be enrolled in France a sufficient proportion of the effective strength of the organizations, so that a cry of alarm could be uttered without the fear of being taxed with exaggeration. Regiments which exist only in skeleton form possess no more than the exterior appearance of a military force.

Leaves at the end of a campaign and the sick-leaves, frequent among the reënlisted men often attacked by the diseases of the tropical countries, make the regimental effectives literally melt away.

Certain regiments have at intervals, an almost laughable strength, on account of the vacancies made by the colonial reliefs. The preparation of the tool indispensable to a nation wishing to have a vast colonial empire must necessarily be the creation of a colonial army. With our system of living from hand to mouth, making the best of a difficulty which presents itself, we have had to deplore too great a mortality; it should be time to reduce it.

§ III. *Departure for the Colonies.*

The time of departing from France and also of arriving in the colony is not indifferent. As far as possible, the men should be made to pass from one climate to the other only at a season when the temperature is about equal in the two countries. The sending of the contingents should be so calculated that the arrivals could take place before winter.

In the Northern hemisphere (Senegal, the Antilles, Indo-China), the most favorable time for the changes would be from January to March; a little before that for Indo-China —from November to January, for example.

For Tong-King, the average duration of the voyage is forty days; by leaving France during the last half of October, the passage through the Suez Canal and the Red Sea will be made at a favorable time; the soldier arrives at his destination in December—that is, in full winter, and during the months of that season which remain he will be able to settle down and become gradually accustomed to the climate.

In Reunion, Madagascar, Guiana, and Oceania, by reason of the reversal of the seasons, the best months to land would be May June, and July.

Reciprocally, the return to France should take place in summer or in spring; but this condition is very difficult to fulfill, especially in the case of the sick, repatriated for urgent reasons.

The influence of a bad season upon the health of those arriving has been too often shown by disastrous examples.

In time of epidemic, every arrival of new troops must be suspended under pain of exposing the new-comers to almost certain death. This is particularly important in case of yellow fever, for the newly arrived men are especially apt to contract it.

The men, after being examined and vaccinated or revaccinated, should always be furnished, before embarking, with their colonial clothing. The hygienic solicitude of the chief of detachment should be exercised during the voyage, when putting into ports, and upon arrival.

His first care, *before departure*, will be to assure himself that each man has a place to sleep and has a hammock; also that he knows how to hang up his nautical bed in a manner to avoid accidents. Then he will make a careful inspection of the linen and clothing of the soldiers, to see if all is in good condition.

During the voyage, bodily cleanliness and the cleanliness of the clothing will be an object of constant watchfulness. The chief of detachment will see that the regulation allowance of soft water for the troops aboard is regularly distributed for their personal use and for the washing of their linen. He will take counsel with the surgeon aboard in case it is necessary to destroy or disinfect the clothing of sick or diseased men. He will also watch the preparation and distribution of the food.

While on board, some occupation for the soldiers is not a bad thing; considering their inexperience of life on the sea, some explanation might be given in regard to the regions traversed.

When the detachment *arrives at its destination*, certain precautions are indispensable. The men will descend into the boats which are to conduct them to land; but the haversacks, arms, and baggage should be lowered separately, so as to avoid accidents.

§ IV. *Time of Sojourn.*

There is no fixed duration of the resistance of the sys

tem in inter-tropical countries. There are great individual differences, greater still according to country.

It is known, nevertheless, that in Cochin-China and Senegal the improved conditions in quartering the troops and the sanitation of the posts have contributed to abate the percentage of mortality, even more than the diminution of the time of sojourn.

Actually, the duration of colonial service is fixed as follows:

Colonies.	Reënlisted.	Reënlisted for More than 3 Years.	Enlisted for 3 Years.
Antilles, Reunion, New Caledonia, Tahiti	4 years.	3 years.	2 years.
Indo-China, Madagascar, Reunion, Senegal, Guiana	3 years.	2 years.	2 years.
Soudan, Bénin	1 year.	1 year.	1 year.

Doctor Navarre finds this idea of *relief at a fixed date* too administrative. It must be acknowledged that, considering the actual conditions of organization it imposes, a uniform sojourn in the colonies would be better.

By carefully examining the study we have made of mortal diseases, the influence of the time of sojourn upon certain affections is apparent; bilious hematuria, sun-stroke, and hepatitis attack a greater proportion of old than of young soldiers, and strike more men at the end than at the beginning of their colonial life. Could this be due to the alcoholic habits unfortunately contracted by too many soldiers, and which are sure to increase with age? That the alcoholic influence upon the genesis of these affections is preponderant is too probable to admit of doubt.

If the new basis of recruitment which we have pointed out were adopted, if there were chosen for the colonies only men fully developed and they were surrounded by all desirable conditions, it is certain that it would be possible to commence increasing the duration of the colonial sojourn, and, according to the colonies, to fix it at five years in the Antilles, Reunion, and Oceania; at three years in Indo-China, Madagascar, Guiana, and Senegal; at eighteen months in the Soudan and Bénin.

In case health should continue excellent, the sojourn could be prolonged in the three-year colonies until the accomplishment of a fourth or fifth year, without ever passing the latter limit; the human system, in fact, needs to renew its strength in the temperate climates after passing a certain time in the torrid climates, if it is not wished to wear it out, and some day have it succumb to the first attack.

Thus, after a maximum sojourn of five years in the colonies, and before, if necessary, every soldier who has not settled in the colony, whether officer or man, should return to France, should go on leave, and then pass, if still in the service, into the district organizations. There he would remain the necessary time, returning to the mobile organizations, ready for a new period of service, only when his health permitted. Sending troops to a very healthy colony, like New Caledonia, after they have served in a less favorable zone like the Soudan, for example, would permit an alternation of the burdens. This would avoid imposing upon anyone in succession, or with an interval of only a year or two, periods of service in an unhealthy place.

This system is, moreover, in use in the case of our colonial functionaries and works well. In default of a better one, we should have recourse to it.

Will we ever be able to go farther in this way? Will it ever be possible to make our soldiers remain in the colonies, like the English in India, for a period of twelve years?

In the present state of our organization, it is difficult to answer in the affirmative; but we have an inmost conviction that when we place our colonial battalions of Tong-King and Madagascar in the health cities, whence they will descend only temporarily—when we surround them with every desirable comfort—nothing will oppose us in imitating our neighbors.

There exist in our new possessions vast regions inhabited by warlike populations, very jealous of their independence, who still regard us as enemies, and who for a long time yet, perhaps, will not resign themselves to our domination. Among them is naturally the place for those groups, imitating the Roman colonies, which M. Brunet has proposed to constitute, and which would be formed of old soldiers provided with lands in recompense for their services, preserving, moreover, a military organization, and ready in case of need, under regularly appointed chiefs, to defend their property and our flag, with arms in hand.

In France, proper attention is far from being given to the utilization of heights for the troops; we believe, however, that it is the most important point in the problem of colonization. The solution is to affirm the possibility of individual acclimatization, and at the same time to definitely settle the question of the colonial army, by assuring to all whom it ought to contain, the primordial condition of every individual, as of every institution—*Life*.

CONCLUSIONS.

Our work would have been vain, and might have been considered aimless, if, after having enumerated the deaths and enunciated the principal causes of mortality among our colonial soldiers, we had made no effort to seek efficacious remedies.

Hygienic statistics relative to service in the Tropics have been given before this, in figures varying between wide extremes; we have reached a just mean, which, far from allaying terror, has dissipated uncertainty by reassuring the pessimists. For the first time, we have arrived at conclusions based upon positive data, and, without caring for reflections which are too optimistic, we have told the truth.

The number of deaths pointed out is accurate, since it has been drawn from the most authentic sources. The average effective strength has been taken as a basis of estimation, and it would be difficult, with the precautions employed, to have more exact information.

In seeking to establish the causes of mortality, and to make out the proportion for each cause, gaps were to be feared; but, in comparing the figures obtained with those of our predecessors, for a century, we have found a reassuring conformity.

The welcome given our first works has shown us that we have been understood and that our manner of seeing and interpreting facts has been appreciated.

It remained for us to show the route to follow to spare the lives of our soldiers; that is the task we have just fulfilled. In approaching this last work, apprehensions have not been wanting. It was necessary to say nothing which had not been studied, long thought of, and profoundly reflected upon; for a false indication might have melancholy consequences.

What we have written has been lived; we have seen what we relate, and the added reflections are stamped with the frankest impartiality.

Our best recompense will be to have done much good, if attention is paid to what we have written.

Among the hygienic measures proposed, there are some which depend upon the man himself, who ought to be powerfully armed for his struggle against the tropical climate.

There are others which depend upon those in command. Those in command can never give too much attention to questions of colonial hygiene, a knowledge of which is as indispensable to them as that of military strategy. Before assuring victory to our arms, is it not necessary to secure life for those who are to give it?

It is primarily from the administration, and still more from the public powers, that one has the right to expect many efforts and great sacrifices. All the questions relative to the recruitment and organization of the colonial troops, to their quartering, equipment, and alimentation, to the cares required by their state of health, in peace as in war, are so many problems whose prompt solution is imposed upon the representatives of the country.

We have pointed out the means best calculated, in our opinion, to hasten the realization of these several desiderata; it is for others to act now. May the statesmen understand the grandeur of the *rôle* devolved upon their patriotism!

If France has hitherto given much gold for the efficacious expansion of her colonial domain, she has also been largely prodigal of the blood of her children!

The hour has come to change all this. Enough corpses have been thrown, sometimes uselessly and without measure, into the balance under pretext of making it incline in our favor; expenses will not be useless, if their end is to preserve lives.

The work of national colonization will prosper only the better for these expenses, and the country will be reconciled to them, without counting the subsidies exacted from it, when it knows that in addition to the price of its glory, it is paying the ransom of the best of its blood.

The End.

MILITARY PUBLICATIONS.

Organization and Tactics. By Lieut.-Colonel Arthur L. Wagner, Assistant Adjutant-General, U. S. Army; late Instructor in the Art of War at the U. S. Infantry and Cavalry School.

This book has been officially adopted as a text-book in the U. S. Engineer School, at Willet's Point, the U. S. Artillery School, at Fort Monroe, the U. S. Infantry and Cavalry School, at Fort Leavenworth, and the U. S. Cavalry and Light Artillery School, at Fort Riley. It has also been officially recommended by the War Department for the use of officers in preparing for examination for promotion.

One volume, 8vo, 514 pages, handsomely bound in blue cloth. (Bound in sheep, 75c extra.) Sent postpaid on receipt of $3.00.

Questions. This pamphlet comprises Appendix III. of Organization and Tactics (second edition), and has been prepared in compliance with the desire expressed by many officers for a list of questions detached from the volume in convenient form for use in preparing for examination. 24-page pamphlet. Sent postpaid on receipt of price, 25c.

The Service of Security and Information. Revised, Enlarged, and with New Illustrations. By Lieut.-Colonel Arthur L. Wagner, Assistant Adjutant-General, U. S. Army; late Instructor in Art of War at the U. S. Infantry and Cavalry School, Fort Leavenworth, Kansas.

This book has been officially adopted by the War Department as a standard in the examination of officers of the Regular Army for promotion. It has also been officially adopted as a text-book in the U. S. Artillery School, Fort Monroe; the U. S. Infantry and Cavalry School, Fort Leavenworth; the U. S. Cavalry and Light Artillery School, Fort Riley.

8vo, 265 pages. Sent postpaid on receipt of $1.50.

A Catechism of Outpost Duty. Including Advance Guard, Rear Guard, and Reconnaissance. By Lieut.-Colonel Arthur L. Wagner, Assistant Adjutant General, U. S. Army; late Instructor in Art of War at the U. S. Infantry and Cavalry School, Fort Leavenworth, Kansas.

This book is a careful abridgment, in the form of questions and answers, of Lieut.-Colonel Wagner's "Service of

HUDSON-KIMBERLY PUBLISHING CO., KANSAS CITY, MO

MILITARY PUBLICATIONS.

Security and Information," which has been officially sanctioned by the War Department as a standard in the examination of officers of the Regular Army for promotion.

One volume, 16mo, cloth, ten illustrative diagrams. Sent postpaid on receipt of 50 cents.

The Campaign of Koniggratz. A study of the Austro-Prussian conflict in the light of the American Civil War. By Lieut.-Col. Arthur L. Wagner. 1 vol., 16mo, with atlas of maps illustrating the theatre of operations and the positions of the opposing armies from the first contact to the end of the decisive battle. Cloth, $2 00.

Military Map-Reading, Field, Outpost and Road Sketching. By Captain W. D. Beach, Instructor in Military Topography at the U. S. Infantry and Cavalry School. 124 pages, full cloth, 75c.

Manual of Military Field Engineering, for the use of Officers and Troops of the Line. Prepared at the U. S. Infantry and Cavalry School by the Department of Engineering. Captain Wm. D. Beach, Third Cavalry, Instructor. Price, $1.75.

Military Topography and Sketching, a Revised Edition, prepared for the Use of the Department of Engineering, United States Infantry and Cavalry School of Fort Leavenworth, by Lieut. Edwin A. Root. 280 pages, full cloth, $2.50.

Horses, Saddles and Bridles. By Maj. William H. Carter, Asst. Adjutant-General, U. S. A. This book has been officially adopted by the War Department as a standard in the examination of officers of the Regular Army for promotion. In the future this publication will be on sale through the Hudson-Kimberly Publishing Co., Kansas City, Mo. Full cloth, 368 pages, illustrated, price, $2 75.

Dickman's Field Holder, with blanks for Road and Position Sketching on Practice Marches, Advance and Rear Guard Duty, Outposts, Relay Lines, and with Instructions for the Men in the Duties of Orderlies and Messengers. Price, 75c; additional Books or Fillers, 25c.

HUDSON-KIMBERLY PUBLISHING CO., KANSAS CITY, MO.

MILITARY PUBLICATIONS.

The Conduct of War. By Lieut.-General von der Goltz, Prussian Army. Full blue cloth, $2.00. Translated by Capt. J. T. Dickman, U. S. A.

A Field Message Book, for the use of Signalists and Army Officers in the field. Designed by Major Howard A. Giddings, Brigade Signal Officer Connecticut National Guard. Cipher disk, pencil, blanks, transfer sheets, and filing pockets, all in a compact water-proof cover. Complete, 75 blanks in pad, compressed-lead pencil. Sent post-paid to any address upon receipt of price, $1.00. Extra pads, 25 cents.

The War Game Simplified, after the method of General Verdy du Vernois. Designed for the use of beginners as well as advanced study of the Military Art. Published with full-sized Maps and complete apparatus for conducting an exercise of the Three Arms Combined. The translation and arrangement are the work of Captain Eben Swift, Fifth Cavalry, formerly in charge of the conduct of the War Game at the United States Infantry and Cavalry School. Price, $5.00.

Infantry Fire; Its Use in Battle. By Jos. B. Batchelor, Jr., First Lieutenant Twenty-fourth United States Infantry. Handsomely bound in leather and complete with tables and illustrations. Sent post-paid upon receipt of price, $2.00.

Notes on the Supply of an Army During Active Operations. By O. Espanet, translated by Capt. H. F. Kendall and Lieut.-Col. Henry G. Sharpe, U. S. A. **The Art of Supplying Armies in the Field as Exemplified During the Civil War.** By Capt. Henry G. Sharpe, Subsistence Department; prize essay from the *Journal of the Military Service Institution of the United States*, 1896. Blue cloth, $2.00.

The Gatling Guns at Santiago. By Lieut. John H. Parker, 13th U. S. Infantry, Commander of the Gatling Gun Detachment at Santiago. Introduction by Col. Theodore Roosevelt, 1st U. S. Volunteer Cavalry (Rough Riders). 300 pages, cloth, octavo, $1.50.

HUDSON-KIMBERLY PUBLISHING CO., KANSAS CITY, MO.

MILITARY PUBLICATIONS.

Tactical Organization and Uses of Machine Guns in the Field. By John H. Parker, First Lieutenant 13th Infantry, Commander of Machine Guns in the Santiago Campaign. 216 pages, blue cloth, $1.50.

Privates' Handbook of Military Courtesy and Guard Duty, being paragraphs from authorized manuals, with changes in manual of arms, saluting, etc., according to recent modifications, and their adaptations to the Springfield arm embodied, and notes. By Lieut. Melvin W. Rowell United States Army, sometime Instructor in Guard Duty and Military Courtesy, Division, National Guard of New Jersey. Price, tag-board cover, 25c; blue cloth, 50c.

Jomini's Life of Napoleon has heretofore been presented in English only in very costly editions; but the edition announced herewith will be sold at the reasonable price of $12.00. This edition is not stereotyped, but is printed from new, clear type, and the edition is limited.

Manual for Cyclists. By Capt. Howard A. Giddings, Brigade Signal Officer, Connecticut National Guard; author of "Instructions in Military Signaling." New Cyclist Drill Regulations, combined with practical instructions for military cyclists, based on extended experiments in this country and abroad. A compendium of valuable information for soldiers using the bicycle. Full blue cloth, illustrated, 96 pages, price, 75c.

Catechismal Edition of the Infantry Drill Regulations, United States Army. Extended Order. General Principles; Leading the Squad; The Squad; The Platoon; The Company; The Battalion; The Regiment; The Brigade in Battle. Prepared by Major Wm. F. Spurgin, 23d Infantry. Price, tag-board cover, 25c; blue cloth, 50c.

The Automatic Instructor. A practical system for home study, adapted for the use of officers in preparing for examination. By Capt. G. W. Read, U. S. A. Blue cloth, 75c.

Regimental Recruiting. By 1st Lieut. F. S. Armstrong (First Cavalry), compiled from Orders and Regulations generally patterned after Circular 7, A. G. O. 1892. Paper, 50c. Blue cloth, 75c.

HUDSON-KIMBERLY PUBLISHING CO., KANSAS CITY, MO

MILITARY PUBLICATIONS.

Customs of the Service. The Army, National Guards, and Volunteers. Compiled from authentic sources by Colonel James W. Powell, United States Army. 200 pages, full blue cloth, $1.50.

English-Spanish Pocket Manual. This Manual is prepared by Lieut. R. G. Hill, 20th Infantry, U. S. A. Vest-pocket size, 80 pages, blue cloth, price, 75c.

Alaska, its History, Climate, Resources, and Wonderful Gold-fields, by Major Henry O. Heistand, Assistant Adjutant-General United States Army. Compiled from the official documents on file in the War, Navy and State Departments, and illustrated by 32 Engravings and 2 large Maps, based on the latest Government surveys by the United States Coast and Geodetic Survey. Sent post-paid for $1.00.

International Military Series.

Edited by
LIEUT.-COLONEL ARTHUR L. WAGNER,
Assistant Adjutant-General, U. S. Army; formerly Instructor in the Art of War at the U. S. Infantry and Cavalry School, Fort Leavenworth, Kansas.

No. 1.
Military Letters and Essays. By Captain F. N. Maude, R.E., author of "Letters on Tactics and Organization," "The Evolution of Modern Drill-Books," etc. 1 volume, 8vo, handsomely bound in blue cloth. Sent postpaid on receipt of $1.50.

No. 2.
Cavalry Studies from Two Great Wars, comprising The French Cavalry in 1870, by Lieutenant-Colonel Bonie (French Army). The German Cavalry in the Battle of Vionville—Mars-la-Tour, by Major Kaehler (German General Staff). The Operations of the Cavalry in the Gettysburg Campaign, by Lieutenant-Colonel George B. Davis, U. S. A. Illustrated; full blue cloth. Sent postpaid on receipt of $1.50.

HUDSON-KIMBERLY PUBLISHING CO., KANSAS CITY, MO.

INTERNATIONAL MILITARY SERIES.

No. 3.

Tactical Studies on the Battles Around Plevna. By Thilo von Trotha, Captain of the Grenadier Regiment Frederic William IV. (Attached.) 1 volume, 8vo, handsomely bound in blue cloth. Sent postpaid on receipt of $1.50.

No. 4.

Cavalry vs. Infantry, and Other Essays. By Captain F. N. Maude, R.E. 1 volume, 8vo, handsomely bound in blue cloth, postpaid, $1.50.

No. 5.

Extracts from an Infantry Captain's Journal on the Trial of a Method for Effectively Training a Company in Skirmishing and Outpost Duty. By Major von Arnim of Hohenzollern Fusilier Regiment No. 40; translated by Major C. J. East, 41st Regiment, D. A. Q. M. G. Full blue cloth, $1.50.

No. 6.

Inquiries into the Tactics of the Future. Developed from Modern Military History by Fritz Hoenig. Translated from the Fourth German Edition by Carl Reichmann, 1st Lieut. 9th Infantry.

The author unites the qualities so desirable in a tactical writer; namely, a deep knowledge of his subject and of human nature, a facility of expression, fearlessness in setting forth his views, and a spirit of philosophical justice, which is shown in giving credit to his enemies as well as bestowing praise upon his friends.

Full blue cloth, 420 pages, price, $2.00.

No. 7.

Hygiene of the Soldier in the Tropics. By F. Burot and M. A. Legrand, translated by Capt. George W. Read, 9th U. S. Cavalry. The importance of a knowledge of Military Hygiene on the part of officers in command of troops has long been recognized, and was painfully emphasized during the war with Spain by the heavy losses of many volunteer organizations that, remaining in home camps, did not see a hostile flag or hear a hostile shot. Blue cloth, postpaid, $1.50.

HUDSON-KIMBERLY PUB. CO., KANSAS CITY, MO.

www.ingramcontent.com/pod-product-compliance
Lightning Source LLC
Chambersburg PA
CBHW031831230426
43669CB00009B/1311